A Beginner's Guide to
SHIP
WATCHING
on the Great Lakes

by Brett Ortler

Adventure Publications
Cambridge, Minnesota

Dedication

To the sailors, past and present, on the Great Lakes.

Acknowledgments

Thanks to the U.S. Coast Guard's Ninth District, and especially Petty Officer 3rd Class Lauren Laughlin and the rest of the Ninth's public affairs staff for their assistance. I also appreciated advice and recommendations from the staff of Mackinac Island State Park, Kenneth Bailey, and Louise Fabris at Fednav. Thanks are also due to the Detroit District of the U.S. Army Corps of Engineers for their many fine public domain photos.

In particular, I want thank Peter Markham of Loretto, Minnesota, for allowing me to use his remarkable photos. You can see more of his fine work at his Flickr site, www.flickr.com/pmarkham, and on his website, www.minnesotageek.net.

Finally, many, many thanks to sailor Doug LaLonde for being kind enough to answer my questions about life aboard ship and for reviewing this book for general accuracy. His blog about serving aboard Great Lakes Vessels (greatlakesships.net) is a must-read.

Cover and book design by Lora Westberg

10 9 8 7 6 5

A Beginner's Guide to Ship Watching on the Great Lakes
Copyright © 2015 by Brett Ortler
Published by Adventure Publications
An imprint of AdventureKEEN
310 Garfield Street South
Cambridge, Minnesota 55008
(800) 678-7006
www.adventurepublications.net
All rights reserved
Printed in China
ISBN 978-1-59193-527-8 (pbk.)

Table of Contents

Introduction

The Great Lakes are home to some of the busier ports in North America, and ship watching is a popular pastime all around the Lakes. It can also be a confusing hobby, because at any given time during shipping season, there are many vessels on the Lakes, and it's hard for a novice to make sense of it all. After all, the shipping industry often seems to speak in a different language (nautical!), and the ships themselves vary in size, construction and cargo. What's more, ships are covered in strange markings and ship watchers refer to terms that can perplex amateurs. (Case in point: Many ship watchers refer to ships on the Great Lakes as "boats," despite the vessels' great size.)

That's why I wrote this book, which is intended as a general intro-duction to ship watching on the Great Lakes. I've included everything a beginner needs, from information about the types of vessels you'll see and what they're carrying to practical advice like the best places to boat watch and how to track your favorite vessels in real-time. (I also snuck in a list of a few especially beautiful ships for you to seek out.) And because shipping and shipwrecks sadly go hand-in-hand, I've included a section about shipwrecks and a few of the more famous wrecks on the Lakes.

Because there are hundreds of ships on the lake, it's not possible to cover every ship in anything other than a cursory manner. I therefore had to be selective; in this book, I outline a few of the major types of vessels, and I then feature a few specific vessels. I chose to feature ships because they were well known, popular, or otherwise inter-esting; this is by no means a slight against the other vessels on the Lakes, their companies, or their crews. Without question, pages and pages could be written about each.

I hope you enjoy this book, and I hope it spurs you to take part in one of the best hobbies in the Great Lakes: ship watching.

The major ports of the Great Lakes, as well as the locks and waterways that make traveling between lakes and to the ocean possible[1, 2]

THUNDER BAY

Lake Superior

Ontario

Minnesota

SILVER BAY

TWO HARBORS

DULUTH

SUPERIOR

MARQUETTE

Michigan

Straits of Mackinac

PORT DOLOMITE

Sault Ste.

MACKINAW CIT

CALCITE   STO

ALPENA

Green Bay

TRAVERSE CITY

Wisconsin

MANISTEE

BAY CITY

Lake Michigan

Michigan   PORT

Lake St.

MILWAUKEE

HOLLAND

DETR

Iowa

CHICAGO

TOLEDO

INDIANA HARBOR · · BURNS HARBOR
GARY

Illinois

Indiana

To the Atlantic Ocean ⟶

Quebec

Saint Lawrence
River

MONTREAL

St. Lambert Lock

Cote Ste.
Catherine Lock

Beauharnois Locks

Eisenhower Lock

Snell Lock

Iroquois Lock

Vermont

Lake
Champlain

Georgian
Bay

Ontario

Lake
Ontario

New York

TORONTO

HAMILTON

BUFFALO

SARNIA

Welland Canal
(and locks)

Lake
Erie

CONNEAUT

ASHTABULA

Pennsylvania

CLEVELAND

Starting Out Ship Watching

Now it's time to actually start ship watching, so bust out your binoculars and let's get started. To do so, just follow these simple steps.

Step 1: Look at the ship's outline.

Unless you're ship watching from a ship lock or in a port, chances are you'll be seeing a ship from a distance, and you'll probably only be able to spot its general outline. That's usually enough to tell you a lot about a ship, though; a ship's design and the equipment on deck can help you identify it.

Use the following guide to identify ships by their outline. Note: Ship design varies, so this is only a general guide for ship spotting. Still, it should be more than enough to get you going.[1]

Lake Freighter (1,000 feet or longer)

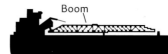

Boom

Engine and pilothouse

Lake Freighter (less than 1,000 feet)

Boom

Pilothouse

Engine

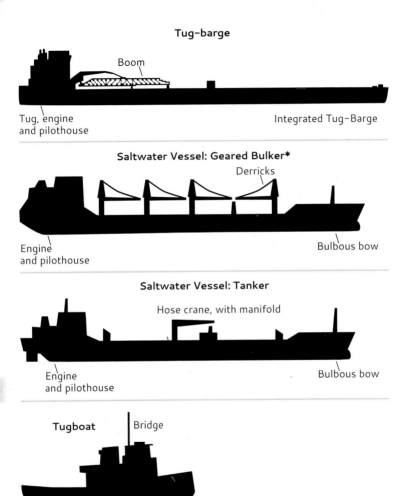

Tug-barge

Boom

Tug, engine
and pilothouse

Integrated Tug-Barge

Saltwater Vessel: Geared Bulker*

Derricks

Engine
and pilothouse

Bulbous bow

Saltwater Vessel: Tanker

Hose crane, with manifold

Engine
and pilothouse

Bulbous bow

Tugboat

Bridge

Engine

*Heavy Lift Ships often look similar but have fewer cranes.

Step 2: Look for flags, and see if you can read the ship's name.

Once you've looked at a ship's outline, look for the flags that it's flying. The flag at the back will tell you the country where the ship is registered.[2] The flag at the front usually represents the country of the port the ship is visiting. If a ship has a pilot on board (all saltwater vessels will), there will be a red–and–white pilot flag flying as well. The pilot flag is part of a special flag–based communication system used in international shipping. Each carries a specific message (or can be used to spell out messages). Generally, signal flags are a rare sight on the Great Lakes, with one exception: ships that are carrying a pilot will display the "Hotel" flag to the right.

Some common flags seen on salties

Liberia

Cyprus

Antigua and Barbuda

Netherlands

Malta

Greece

International Signal Flags Alphabet

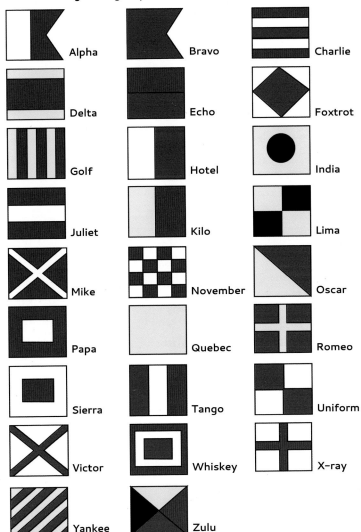

Alpha

Bravo

Charlie

Delta

Echo

Foxtrot

Golf

Hotel

India

Juliet

Kilo

Lima

Mike

November

Oscar

Papa

Quebec

Romeo

Sierra

Tango

Uniform

Victor

Whiskey

X-ray

Yankee

Zulu

Step 3: Check the ship's stack markings and paint scheme.

Once you've checked the flag, take a look at the ship's smokestacks and its paint scheme. Most companies paint their ships in a specific color scheme, and each has its own stack marking—a combination of colors and geometric shapes; some also feature company logos. As you gain experience ship watching, you'll start to identify each company's ships by the paint and stack markings alone.[3] Here are the stack markings of the big three U.S. companies. For their paint schemes, see the next page.

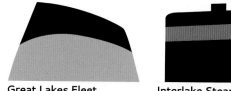

Great Lakes Fleet

Interlake Steamship Company

American Steamship Company

Step 4: Look the ship up online.

Once you've spotted the ship, look the ship up online via one of the many ship watching sites. Sites like www.marinetraffic.com and Boatnerd's AIS site (ais.boatnerd.com) track a ship's Automated Identification Signal (AIS), giving you its current location, heading, last port of call, and so on.[4, 5] (And if you know the ship and where it's headed, you can usually make a good guess about its cargo.) This gives you a real-time look at where a ship is, and where it is headed. You can even create your own "fleet" of ships, in order to track your favorites.

Great Lakes Fleet

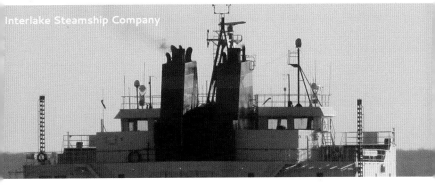
Interlake Steamship Company

American Steamship Company

SHIP WATCHING FAQ

In all, there are 85 U.S. ports on the Great Lakes, and they dot the shoreline of every state bordering the Great Lakes.[1] This means that there are dozens and dozens of places to ship watch. And some of them are quite busy ports, making them perfect places to ship watch. To get started, check out the frequently asked questions pages that follow, as they'll give you a quick introduction to Great Lakes ship watching.

The *American Courage*

The Basics

Where should I go ship watching?

Everyone has their favorite places to ship watch on the Lakes, but if you're looking to consistently see ships, you need to do two things: one, track your favorite ships online (see page 174) and two, visit areas that are frequented by many ships. Ships travel on the Great Lakes thanks to series of locks, channels and other man-made systems. The St. Lawrence Seaway consists of many "funnel points" where all ships must travel, and the Seaway's many locks, rivers and canals are therefore great places to boatwatch.[1] The same goes for parks and public areas near busy ports.

When is the best time to see ships?

Because lake freighters are always on the move, ship schedules are anything but predictable, so planning a vacation around ship watching can be a risky proposition. The best way to ensure you see ships is to keep track of the ships online (see page 174) and by vacationing near the primary locks, canals and channels where ships have to pass through.[2] For specific advice on places to visit, see page 50.

What's a laker? What's a saltie?

Lakers are U.S. or Canadian bulk freighters that travel on the Great Lakes. U.S. lakers stay on the Great Lakes, whereas some Canadian ships split their time between the Great Lakes and coastal areas on the Atlantic coast. Salties are foreign vessels that enter the Great Lakes via the St. Lawrence Seaway.

Do ocean-going vessels travel on the Great Lakes?

You read that right. Ocean-going vessels can travel on the Great Lakes thanks to the St. Lawrence Seaway, a system of locks, channels and waterways that helps ships bypass natural hazards, such as Niagara Falls. The Seaway system connects Lake Ontario and Lake Erie to the Atlantic Ocean, enabling ships up to 740 feet long to travel from lake to lake. If ships are any bigger, they don't fit in the locks that help move ships from lake to lake.[3] A long series of other locks, channels and canals allows ships to travel to the rest of the Great Lakes.

How far can ocean-going ships travel on the Great Lakes?

At 2,342 miles from the Atlantic Ocean, the twin ports of Duluth–Superior are the farthest inland freshwater ports, and they receive over 1,000 vessels each year. To reach the Great Lakes, ships

The *Rt. Hon. Paul J. Martin* entering Duluth Harbor

must traverse the Saint Lawrence Seaway, an engineering marvel that allows ocean-going ships to travel through all of the Great Lakes. Starting in the St. Lawrence River (which connects to the Gulf of St. Lawrence on the Atlantic), there is a series of locks near Montreal that allows ships to travel through the St. Lawrence River, which eventually reaches Lake Ontario. From there, the ships traverse the smallest Great Lake, before reaching another series of locks and the Welland Canal, a man-made canal that bypasses Niagara Falls. After passing through the Welland Canal, ships proceed through Lake Erie, into Lake Huron, eventually leading to Sault Ste. Marie, Michigan, where ships must pass through the Soo Locks to reach Lake Superior.[4] (All of the locks and channels after the Welland Canal aren't technically part of the St. Lawrence Seaway proper, but for our purposes, it's one continuous system.)

The locks of the St. Lawrence Seaway are huge—766 feet long—but some ships are simply too big to fit. The maximum size a ship can be and still fit in the locks is known as "Seawaymax"; Seawaymax ships can't exceed 740 feet in length, or 78 feet in width, so any ship longer or wider can't travel from Lake Erie to Lake Ontario. This means that the ships in excess of 740 feet are confined to life on the upper four Great Lakes (Superior, Michigan, Huron, Erie).

Anatomy of a Great Lakes Vessel

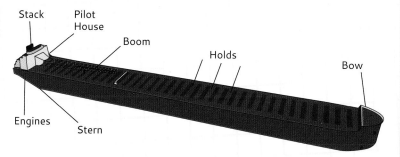

Stack · Pilot House · Boom · Holds · Bow · Engines · Stern

How long are most ships?

Ocean-going ships have to pass through the St. Lawrence Seaway; it can only accept ships up to 740 feet long. Many cargo ships on the Great Lakes are much larger, however. The largest class of ships—the thousand footers—are over a thousand feet long.

What's the biggest ship on the Lakes?

At 1,013.5 feet, the *Paul R. Tregurtha* is the biggest ship on the Lakes.[5] As the largest ship on the Lakes, she is known informally as "Queen of the Lakes."

What do ships on the Great Lakes carry?

U.S. and Canadian vessels usually carry iron ore, coal, limestone or other stone products, grain products or cement. Ocean-going ships carry all sorts of cargo, including heavy equipment and even massive wind turbine blades.[6]

How fast does a lake freighter go?

It varies by ship, but most ships have a maximum speed somewhere around 18 miles per hour. They usually travel a bit slower than that, at around 12–15 miles per hour.[7]

How much weight can a lake freighter carry?

A single 1000–footer can carry tens of thousands of tons of material. For example, the *Indiana Harbor* regularly carries well over 50,000 tons of cargo on each trip, the equivalent of the weight of over 8,000 elephants.

How many horsepower do the engines have?

Larger ships have more horsepower. The 1000–footers have diesel engines that combined can produce at least 14,000 horsepower; some have engines that can produce up to 19,500 horsepower.[8]

How long is the life of a typical saltie?

Because saltwater is incredibly corrosive, it takes a toll on a ship's hull; saltwater vessels usually don't last longer than two decades.

How long is the life of a typical laker?

Freshwater is much less corrosive than saltwater, so ships on the Great Lakes last much longer than ocean–going vessels. It's not uncommon for a ship to serve for over half a century, and sometimes much longer. The *St. Marys Challenger* served from 1906 to 2013; now converted to a barge, her hull is still in service on the Lakes.

How does the cost of shipping compare with trucking or flying?

Because they transport a huge quantity of material at once, ships are far more efficient than any other variety of transportation. One 1000–footer carries the same amount of cargo as six mile–long trains or more than 2,000 semi–trailers.[9]

Can I ride on a Laker?

Lakers aren't certified to carry paying passengers, so the only way to ride on one is to win a raffle. Raffles are held by the shipping companies every so often, with the proceeds usually going to area charities. To find a raffle, visit the best ship watching site on the web: www.boatnerd.com. They often list raffles on their site.

The *Sam Laud* near Two Harbors

Types of Ships

If you get close to a lake freighter, you'll see that ships have a variety of markings on them. These markings communicate important information to the captain and crew, and to workers in harbors, canals and locks.

What's a lake freighter?

A lake freighter is a Great Lakes vessel dedicated to carrying bulk cargo. There are two primary types: self-unloading vessels and bulk freighters without equipment (often called straight deckers). Self-unloading ships are exactly what you'd expect—once they get to port, they are equipped with a conveyor belt system and a boom to unload their cargo without the assistance of support staff on shore.[1] Nearly all lakers in the American Fleet on the Great Lakes are self-unloaders, as they are much more efficient and cost-effective than relying on equipment and staff at port. (This makes sense, given that the American fleet also boasts the largest ships.) Because straight deckers lack equipment necessary to unload their cargo when arriving at port, this means they are dependent on shore-based equipment and staff.[2] A rarity in the U.S. fleet, the Canadian fleet includes a number of straight deckers.[3]

What's a tug-barge?

Once somewhat rare on the Great Lakes, tug-barges are now something of a trendy option when it comes to Great Lakes ship-building.[4] Tug-barges consist of two different sections: a barge that carries cargo and a dedicated tugboat that is attached to the ship, allowing it to propel the barge. These ships sail as one vessel; the two components are not intended to separate when in transit. There are two kinds of tug–barges: integrated tugs, which have no range of motion when attached to a vessel, and articulated tugs, which can move on one axis. So why were these ships built at all? As they aren't a full-fledged laker, they require a smaller crew, making them cheaper to operate.[5]

What's a tugboat?

The workhorses of the Great Lakes, tugboats do everything from help ships dock to pull barges and break ice. Tugs are essentially floating engines, and they often boast over 1,000 horsepower.[6, 7] Tugs were also built to last; many of the tugs in service on the Great Lakes were built in the early twentieth century; one tug currently on the water—the *Jill Marie*— was built in 1891.[8]

The *American Integrity* in Duluth

What's a saltie?

Foreign ships that ply the Great Lakes are known as "salties" because they travel to the Great Lakes from the Atlantic Ocean via the St. Lawrence Seaway. There are three general types of salties: bulk carriers, lift ships and tankers.

Like the bulk carriers of the U.S. and Canadian fleets, salties that are bulk carriers carry large amounts of one type of cargo on each trip. U.S.-flagged vessels are often dedicated to a particular kind of cargo (iron ore or coal, for instance) and sometimes visit the same ports again and again. By comparison, the cargo of saltwater bulk carriers varies significantly. While salties often carry iron ore and coal, they also transport a variety of other materials, including salt, cement and stone; when they drop off their cargo, they often pick up a new one for the return voyage.

Lift ships carry exceptionally heavy, bulky cargo and are equipped with the cranes necessary to move it. Common cargoes include wind turbine blades and nacelles, electrical transformers and other heavy equipment.[9]

Tankers carry large amounts of liquids; petroleum products are the most common cargoes, but other chemicals are shipped as well.

Is there a Coast Guard presence on the Lakes?

The U.S. Coast Guard maintains a fleet of 10 cutters that serve on the Great Lakes.[10] They range in size from the 240-foot *Mackinaw* to the 100-foot *Buckthorn*.[11] The Coast Guard also operates a fleet of smaller vessels and a number of planes and helicopters. The Coast Guard plays myriad roles on the Lakes—its ships serve as icebreakers, maintain shipping canals and serve as search-and-rescue vessels, and they also monitor and maintain navigational markers, buoys and the like. (For more about the Coast Guard, see page 132.)

What other vessels are seen on the Lakes?

The Lakes are home to a wide variety of other vessels, including everything from fishing vessels and sailboats to sightseeing cruisers. The Lakes can even boast occasional visits by "tall ships," traditional sailing vessels (think: pirate ship) that are always a crowd favorite.[12]

U.S. Coast Guard vessel *Sundew*

The U.S. & Canadian Fleets

Where do the majority of cargo ships on the Great Lakes come from?

Given that the U.S. and Canada both border the Great Lakes, chances are, most of the vessels you'll see are either from Canada or the U.S. Both countries boast large cargo fleets, though they differ in a number of important ways.

How many ships are in the U.S. fleet?

The U.S. fleet consists of nearly 60 vessels, almost all of which are large, bulk cargo–carrying vessels.[1] The U.S. fleet boasts the largest vessels on the Great Lakes. All of the 1000-footers on the Lakes are operated by U.S. companies.[2] Because well-made hulls can last for decades, many of the vessels in the U.S. fleet are several decades old (or older). Nonetheless, a few new vessels (tug–barge combinations) have been constructed recently.[3]

What kind of ships are in the U.S. fleet?

With a few exceptions, there are two types of vessels in the U.S. fleet: self-unloading bulk carriers or tug–barge combinations. Self-unloading cargo vessels are exactly what they sound like: cargo vessels that carry equipment that allows them to "self-unload" when they reach port. This equipment usually consists of a large boom (which rests on the deck while the ship is at sea) and a conveyor belt system beneath the holds. Tug–barge combinations are a little different; they consist of a large barge that is propelled by a custom-made tug that fits into a slot at the end of the barge.

Unlike normal tugboats, these tugboats aren't well suited to pulling a vessel or nudging it into position. Instead, they stay "mated" with their barges for the voyage and sail as a single ship.

How many ships are in the Canadian fleet?

With nearly 70 vessels, the Canadian laker fleet is larger than the U.S. fleet.[4] A number of new Canadian vessels have been built lately, including a new class of cargo vessel, the Trillium class.[5]

What kind of ships are in the Canadian fleet?

Like their American counterparts, Canadian vessels carry large amounts of bulk cargo, but the Canadian fleet is much more varied. All of its ships are less than 740 feet long, enabling them to travel via the St. Lawrence Seaway. In addition, while most are bulk freighters, the Canadian fleet also boasts a number of tankers.[6]

The *Algosoo*

U.S. Ports & Cargo

There are thirty-seven major U.S. ports on the Great Lakes, as well as dozens of important Canadian ports, so it's difficult to cover them all.[1] Nonetheless, a brief look at the busiest ports and the cargoes they traffic in can tell you a lot about the ships you're seeing—and what they might be carrying.

What do ships on the Great Lakes carry?

Great Lakes freighters are built to do one thing: carry large amounts of bulk cargo in their holds. The term "bulk cargo" means a large amount of unpackaged cargo. Examples of bulk cargo include coal, iron ore, or grain.[2] This cargo is all loaded into the ship's holds. When the ship arrives at port, it's off-loaded, almost always with the help of the ship's onboard equipment (conveyor belts and the like). Then the ship leaves to pick up another load of cargo. This process continues 24 hours a day, seven days a week, during the shipping season.

What are the primary bulk cargoes?

There are three primary cargoes carried by the U.S. Great Lakes fleet: iron ore (also known as taconite), coal and limestone.[3] Taken together, they represent the vast majority of the cargo hauled by U.S. ships.

Where does the iron ore shipped on the Lakes come from and how is it used?

Iron ore is the most popular commodity shipped on the Great Lakes. The majority of the iron-ore shipped on the Great Lakes comes from Minnesota's Mesabi Iron Range, but iron is also shipped from northern Michigan's Marquette Iron Range. Today, much of the iron ore on the Great Lakes takes the form of taconite, a low-grade iron ore, consisting of approximately 20—30 percent iron.[4] The taconite is crushed into small pieces and then ground into powder. The iron is removed with the help of high-powered magnets. This iron, which takes the form of a powder, is then mixed with water and clay, so it forms a small marble-like sphere. This produces a finished taconite pellet, and each consists of something like 65 percent iron.[5] These pellets are shipped by rail to Minnesota's and Michigan's ports, where they are loaded onto lakers and sent "down" the Lakes to mills in Michigan, Indiana and Ohio, where the pellets are refined and used to make steel.

The Hull-Rust-Mahoning Mine, in Minnesota

Where does the coal shipped on the Great Lakes come from? Where does it go?

The second-most shipped commodity on the Lakes, coal on the Great Lakes primarily comes from two places—the Appalachian Mountain Range and the Powder River Basin of Montana and Wyoming.[6] This coal differs significantly: much of the coal reserves from the western U.S. are significantly lower in sulfur content, making it a popular choice overseas, as a higher sulfur content leads to more pollution.[7, 8] While iron ore is shipped predominantly from ports on Lake Superior "down" to the other lakes, coal is shipped up the Lakes and down the Lakes as circumstances merit. While it might seem strange that the same ports are receiving and shipping coal, coal-fired power plants are sprinkled throughout the Great Lakes region, so coal is often in significant demand.

Why is limestone shipped? Where does it go?

Quarried in Michigan and Ohio, limestone is an essential material for road construction and it is also used in cement and steel production and manufacturing.[9] It is shipped from the central Great Lakes region throughout all of the Great Lakes. Because limestone contains a significant amount of water and is washed prior to shipment, it can be damaged by cold weather, so its shipping season is slightly shorter.[10]

Are there less-common cargoes?

Cement, salt, sand and gravel, and some agricultural products are also shipped on the Lakes, but these cargoes only account for a fraction of the total cargo shipping on the Great Lakes in the U.S. Nonetheless, that doesn't mean these cargoes are unimportant. On the contrary, given the vast cargo capacity of just one lake freighter, vast amounts of these "minor" cargoes are still moved. For example, in 2009, "only" 656,420 tons of grain-based products were shipped domestically on the Lakes.[11] Still, that's enough to fill over nine 1000-foot lake freighters.

To put that in perspective, a fully loaded laker holds 2 million bushels of wheat.[12] Given that a bushel of wheat is enough to make 90 loaves of whole wheat bread, the wheat in one laker could make 180 million loaves of bread.[13]

What are the busiest ports?

The twin ports of **Duluth-Superior** are the busiest on the Lakes, receiving over 1,000 vessels each year.[14] The primary cargoes shipped at Duluth are iron-ore (from the nearby Mesabi Iron Range in Minnesota) and coal (shipped by rail from the western U.S.) Many salties visit Duluth to take on loads of grain, as well.

Entrance to the Port of Duluth

The **Port of Chicago** is actually a collection of several related ports, and the second-busiest port on the Lakes. The busiest general cargo port, it's a hub for intermodal shipping—shipping that occurs via the familiar shipping containers on semi trucks and trains.[15]

Consisting of three separate ports, the **Ports of Indiana** ship a wide variety of cargo. Of U.S. ports, Burns Harbor ships the most ocean-going cargo on the Great Lakes, as well as about 15 percent of U.S. steel exports to Europe.[16]

Not far from the port of Duluth-Superior, **Two Harbors** primarily exports iron ore from Minnesota's Iron Range, regularly shipping over 13 million tons of cargo each year.[17]

Detroit is a major center for automobile construction and steel-making, so Detroit's port is regularly busy with loads of iron ore. It also sees shipments of coal (for nearby power plants) and limestone, which is used in construction (and in the steelmaking process).[18]

Cleveland is home to a number of steelmaking facilities, so it's no surprise that it receives many shipments of iron ore, limestone and other products that go into steel production. It's the seventh-busiest port (after nearby Toledo, which is #6).[19]

Canadian Ports: Canada also boasts a series of incredibly important ports, including Montreal, Quebec, Toronto and Windsor, among others. Because Canada's ports are often visited by vessels that pass through the St. Lawrence Seaway to the Atlantic, Canadian cargoes are often more diversified. While iron ore and coal are still common cargoes, Canadian ships load and unload everything from wheat and other agricultural products to fuel oils and chemicals.

Are there other ports on the Great Lakes?

Dozens! That's the really amazing thing about ship watching on the Great Lakes: Great Lakes freighters visit ports all over the Lakes, and this means there are that many different towns to visit and vistas to photograph. A "Grand Tour" of the Great Lakes ports is really a tour of the Lakes.

An aerial view of Two Harbors, MN

Foreign Ships

How can I tell which country a ship is from?

Many foreign-flagged vessels visit the Great Lakes each year. On each one, the country of origin is printed on the stern (back) of the ship. The flag of its country of registration flies at the back of the ship as well.[1]

What's a country of registration? Why are there so many flags from countries I don't recognize?

Many companies choose to register their ships in a different country in order to avoid the laws and restrictions imposed by their home countries. So it's not uncommon to find a ship owned by a Canadian company that is registered in Cyprus or another "port of convenience."[2] Common examples include Liberia, Cyprus, Malta and the Marshall Islands.[3]

When this happens, the ship flies the flag of the country of registration at the stern of the ship. Many foreign vessels also fly the flag of the country they are visiting at the bow of the ship.

What kind of foreign ships can be seen on the Great Lakes?

The foreign-flagged fleet on the Great Lakes is more diverse than the U.S.-Canada fleets. While most foreign vessels are still bulk cargo carriers, foreign-flagged vessels vary both in terms of their design and their cargoes. Foreign vessels range from familiar bulk cargo ships to more unusual vessels, like lift ships and chemical carriers.[4]

Do foreign ships carry different cargo?

On their way here, yes. To make a trip worthwhile, most vessels arrive on the Great Lakes bearing a load of cargo, then return bearing cargo from the Great Lakes. They bring a wide variety of cargoes to the region, everything from wind turbine blades to the familiar shipping containers often seen on railroad cars.

How many foreign ships are there on the Great Lakes?

The number of vessels on the Lakes varies significantly by year and economic conditions. Sometimes, individual foreign vessels visit relatively regularly, whereas some vessels are only seen once.

The *Olza*, a saltie

Understanding Ship Whistles

Why do ships blow their whistles before they leave?

This is pretty common. One short blast means: Cast off the lines. This indicates that the ship is getting ready to leave. So, if you're enjoying watching a ship that is getting ready to leave, be aware that a whistle blast is probably coming.[1]

Two ships approached each other, then blew their whistles. What were they saying?

When a ship is underway and is approaching another ship and both are headed toward each other, one short blast means: I am altering my course to starboard (right). Two short blasts means: I am altering my course to port (left). If the other ship agrees, they respond with the same signal.[2]

A ship was approaching another one from behind and honked. Why?

When a ship wants to pass another ship, one short blast means: I intend to overtake you on your starboard side. Two short blasts means: I intend to overtake you on your port side. (If the other ship agrees, they respond with the same signal.)[3]

Why do ships sound their whistles in fog?

For safety reasons, ships have to signal one blast every two minutes when in fog.[4]

What does five quick whistle blasts mean?

Five quick blasts means "danger." Hopefully, you'll never hear this signal![5]

Why do two passing ships sometimes blast their whistles?

When a captain wants to say "hello" to another captain, they do so with one long blast, followed by two short blasts: This is the customary way that captains say hello to each other.[6]

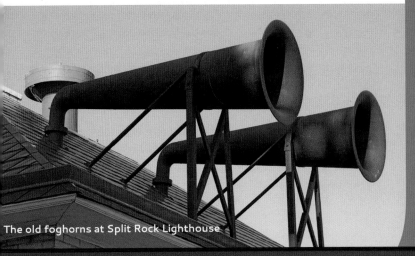

The old foghorns at Split Rock Lighthouse

Ship Markings

If you get close to a lake freighter, you'll see that ships have a variety of markings on them. These markings communicate important information to the captain and crew, and to workers in harbors, canals and locks.

Why are there numbers on the front of a ship?

The most obvious markings are draft marks on the ship's bow, which indicate the distance between the waterline and the bottom of the ship. This is important because a ship's draft is affected by its cargo. If a ship has more cargo, it sinks deeper into the water. The St. Lawrence Seaway is only dredged to a depth of 27 feet, so there is not much margin for error, especially for the biggest ships.

Why do some ships have a propeller-like marking at the front and the back?

This marking indicates that a ship has a bow or stern thruster, which is essentially a propeller that helps the ship maneuver more effectively. These propellers have become increasingly popular, much to the chagrin of tugboat captains (whose work they replace). These markings help keep port staff safe; if a thruster is engaged, it can cause part of the ship to move more quickly than with just the engine engaged.

What's that strange marking on the side of a ship?

The Plimsoll Line is a funny-looking set of lines and squiggles, but it's incredibly important, as it indicates the maximum depth for a ship in a number of different water conditions (freshwater, tropical, summer, winter, etc.). If a ship exceeds that depth (and the Plimsoll line is underwater), the ship is exceeding its capacities and is in danger. The line is named for Samuel Plimsoll, a British Member of Parliament in the nineteenth century who pushed for standardized shipping marks to prevent overloading on ships.[1]

Why do some ocean-going ships have a funny symbol on their bow that sort of looks like a bulbous nose?

This indicates that the ship has a bulbous bow. A bulbous bow lowers a ship's drag at high speeds.[2] This design addition is especially useful for ocean-going ships, so you'll often see it on salties.

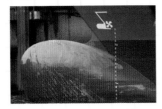

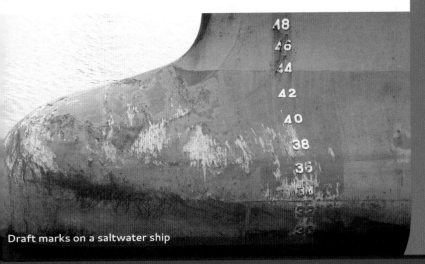

Draft marks on a saltwater ship

Stack Markings & Color Schemes

What are those markings on a ship's smokestack?

Each shipping company has its own unique smokestack markings; these markings consist of a combination of shapes and letters that identify which company the ship belongs to. It's perhaps easiest to think of them as something like a family crest.[1]

These are the stack markings for some of the largest U.S.-flagged fleets on the lake. They are just a few examples of stack markings that you might see on the Great Lakes.

Why are ships painted in different colors?

Just as each company has its own stack markings, each company usually has a specific paint scheme for its ships. The more you boatwatch, the more you'll start to recognize the varying paint schemes, making it much easier to identify ships.

Note: Vessels change hands periodically and painting a vessel is an expensive proposition, so paint schemes aren't a definitive way to identify a ship. Here are the paint schemes for the three largest U.S.-flagged fleets.

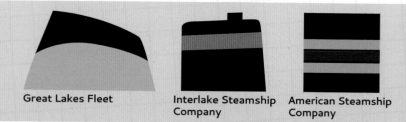

Great Lakes Fleet

Interlake Steamship Company

American Steamship Company

Great Lakes Fleet: A mostly red hull interrupted by a wide gray swath and a smaller black one near the bow.[2]

Interlake Steamship Company: A red hull with a white deck/superstructure.[3]

American Steamship Company: A mostly black hull with a white line around the stern.[4]

Navigation

How do ships navigate on the Great Lakes?

Navigation has come a long way since the early days of commerce and exploration on the Great Lakes. Back then, mariners had little more than a compass, charts, and a few visual aids to navigation to help guide them. Like their forebears, today's mariners are incredibly well trained and experienced, but they also have access to a variety of high-tech tools, including GPS, electronic nautical charts, radio and radar. Of course, the ships also carry more old-fashioned tools, like paper nautical charts, and their crews often reference aids to navigation like buoys, beacons, range markers, harbor lights and lighthouses.[1]

Some examples of aids to navigation (buoys)[2]

I've heard the phrase "upbound" and "downbound." What do they mean?

When freighters travel on the Great Lakes, they do so in dedicated shipping lanes. These lanes, which were naturally gouged out by the glaciers, offer a deepwater passage across nearly the entirety of the Great Lakes. To alleviate traffic congestion and make things safer, there are dedicated lanes for each direction of travel. Ships heading west, and "up" the Lakes, are considered "upbound" and travel in a dedicated shipping lane. Ships heading "downbound," toward the Atlantic Ocean, also travel in a designated lane.[3] These routes are often called "LCA" routes and get their name from the Lake Carriers' Association, the group that represents all of the U.S. cargo carriers on the Lakes.

What's the Automatic Identification System?

Each freighter on the Great Lakes is outfitted with equipment that sends data to the Automatic Identification System.[4] This system collects position data from every ship on the Lakes, and gives mariners a real-time view of all ships on the Lakes. The system, which updates automatically every few seconds, makes travel on the Lakes much safer. Thanks to sites such as marinetraffic.com, AIS also enables ship watchers to see which ships are near them at any given time. This makes AIS an absolutely indispensable tool for ship watching.

How do ships communicate with one another?

The primary way ships communicate is via radio, and there are dedicated frequencies for inter-ship communications, distress signals and port operations. All ships carrying radio are also required to tune in to the emergency channel in order to provide assistance if possible. If necessary, ships can also communicate by sounding their whistles, using shipboard lights, or by hoisting signal flags.[5]

How long does it take for a ship to reach its destination?

While travel times obviously vary based on destination, it usually only takes a few days for a vessel to reach port.[6] This travel time includes passage through canals and locks, which often take some time to pass through because of speed limits. If this sounds surprisingly fast, remember that vessels travel at a fairly high speed and are always on the move.

How long does the shipping season last on the Great Lakes?

The shipping season on the Great Lakes depends on weather conditions and usually begins in the end of March or early April and lasts until January.

Do the Great Lakes freeze over in the winter?

Sometimes. While some ice cover is normal (and expected), sometimes one or more of the Great Lakes will freeze over. In exceptional winters, nearly all of the Great Lakes can freeze over. When this happens, the ice often takes some time to break up, delaying the start of the shipping season, and forcing the Coast Guard to operate icebreakers to open up shipping lanes. In the worst years, this leads to pronounced delays, causing trips that usually take three days to last for weeks.[7]

Where do the ships go in the winter?

During the winter, Great Lakes freighters enter "winter layup" at a shipyard, where they undergo repairs and upgrades in preparation for the coming shipping season. Ships are also periodically inspected for seaworthiness by the Coast Guard.

What are pilots? How do I know if a ship has a pilot aboard?

Some areas—channels and harbors, for instance—are hard to navi-gate. Pilots are expert navigators who come aboard to specifically guide ships through such areas. The captains of U.S. and Canadian vessels already qualify as pilots, and the same usually goes for deck officers, so an additional pilot isn't needed, but saltwater vessels all require pilots when sailing on the Great Lakes. When pilots come aboard, the ship will raise a pilot's flag, which indicates a pilot is on board.[8] When you see a number of saltwater vessels waiting in a harbor, they are often waiting for pilots.

The *Indiana Harbor* near Cleveland

Life Aboard Ship

How many crew members are on a Great Lakes vessel?

It varies by ship, but most U.S. vessels have somewhere around 21—27 crew members[1]. Integrated tug–barges (see page 104) are the exception; this newer type of ship is something of a trend and consists of a tug that is fitted in a notch in the barge's hull. The ship sails as one vessel and has a crew that's about a third smaller than that of a typical Great Lakes vessel.

What do the various crew members do?

There are three primary types of jobs on a ship: crew members either work in the deck department (the bridge), in the engine room, or in the galley (kitchen).[2] The captain oversees the crew members in the pilothouse as they guide the ship along its course. These crew members, including the captain, are qualified as pilots, which means they are licensed to steer/navigate a Great Lakes vessel. Depending on their rank, they also have a wide variety of other duties, including overseeing loading and unloading, maintaining the ship's log, taking care of administrative paperwork, and even keeping track of supplies for the ship.[2] The crew in the engine room maintains the engine and assists when unloading, and the kitchen staff keeps the crew fed and helps boost morale.[3]

Where do crews come from?

Because of a U.S. law known as the Jones Act, all U.S.-flagged lake freighters are required to have crews from the U.S., so if you see a U.S.-flagged ship, its crew members are likely from around the Great Lakes. Ships from Canada or from overseas do not have the same requirements, so their crews are considerably more diverse. It's not unheard of to have a German-owned ship with a European crew on a Liberian-flagged ship.

What's the difference between an officer, an able seaman, and a mate?

When it comes to titles aboard ship, things can be tricky. Generally speaking, on Great Lakes vessels, there are three types of crew members: officers, able seamen and ordinary seamen.

A ship's officers include the captain, all pilots (deck officers who are also known as mates), the chief engineer, and assistant engineers.

The U.S. Coast Guard administers examinations for officers and able seamen.[5] There are two ways to obtain a license or an endorsement: candidates can graduate from a merchant marine academy or they can work as unlicensed seamen and gain experience and then take the required examinations to become an able seaman.

JAMES R. BARKER

The *James R. Barker* entering Duluth

Crew members who don't hold a Coast Guard license or endorsement are called seamen. Those without any additional endorsements from the Coast Guard are called "ordinary seamen." Some ordinary seamen are certified in other areas. One example is the Qualified Member of the Engine Department certification.

What are bedrooms/sleeping accommodations like?

It depends on the ship, but most sailors have their own room. Rooms can vary considerably. Some ships were built to impress clients, who were expected to travel onboard the ship. Such vessels, the *Paul R. Tregurtha* among them, have stately rooms with elaborate wood paneling.[6] Other vessels are far less showy. When it comes to creature comforts, most newer vessels have air conditioning, and crew members often have access to the Internet, and a break room/lounge.

What are the working hours on a Great Lakes ship?

Because freighters operate continuously during the shipping season, the working hours are hardly 9 to 5.[7] Instead, crew members serve shifts of four hours on, followed by eight hours off. There are three possible shifts: 4—8, 8—12 or 12—4. A crew member with a shift of 4—8 would be on duty from 4 to 8 a.m. and 4 to 8 p.m. They'd be off duty from 8 a.m. to 4 p.m. and 8 p.m to 4 a.m.

What do crew members do during their downtime?

Sleeping and eating are obvious pastimes, but sailors also watch television, read, surf the Internet, or play cards or video games.

How safe is working on a Great Lakes vessel?

Shipping on the Great Lakes was once a pretty dangerous business, and in the early days of sail-powered vessels, it wasn't uncommon for a dozen or more ships to be lost in a shipping season. Today, shipwrecks are mercifully rare; the last major wreck to occur on the Great Lakes was the loss of the *Edmund Fitzgerald* in 1975. That doesn't mean that there are no dangers, however. Shipwrecks are still possible, of course, but more everyday problems like slips and falls are more common complaints. Deaths on Great Lakes vessels are very rare, and most are usually due to natural causes.[8]

Where else do foreign ships go?

All over! Keeping track of saltwater vessels is an interesting hobby in its own right, and thanks to the AIS system (see page 174), you can track a "saltie" after it has left the Great Lakes. A ship that visited the Great Lakes might turn up on the North Sea or even farther afield.

The *Isadora*, a saltie

WHERE TO SHIP WATCH

At its core, ship watching is simple, a spectator sport. Most beginners don't care about engine configurations or want to decipher a ship's stack markings. Instead, they want to know the very basics: where to see boats and what to expect. If that's what you want, read on. Here you'll find information about some of the finest ship watching destinations on each of the Great Lakes, including nearby nautical-themed attractions and real-time ship-tracking websites to help you know which ships are near you. I also include the occasional ship watching site that is a hidden gem. Because there are dozens of ports and thousands of places to boatwatch on the Lakes, this list is hardly all-inclusive, but it should definitely get you started!

The *Edgar B. Speer*

Lake Superior

Duluth, MN, and Superior, WI

Commonly referred to as the "Twin Ports" because of their proximity to one another, together Duluth and Superior are the busiest U.S. ports on the lake. Thousand-foot-long vessels are a common sight in the area, which also boasts an abundance of ship watching locations.

Canal Park is the most popular ship watching location in Duluth. A beautiful park bordering the Lake Superior shore, Canal Park offers stunning views of Duluth as well as an up-close look at ships entering the harbor, thanks to the famous Aerial Lift Bridge. All vessels entering the harbor have to pass under the lift bridge, which rises up to a maximum height of 226 feet, providing nearly 140 feet of clearance, enough to let even the tallest lake freighters pass through.[1] There's nothing quite like seeing a 1000-foot vessel pass under the raised lift bridge; better yet, because the shipping canal is relatively narrow, you get an up-close-and-personal view of the vessels. How close? The ships' crews are often on deck and wave to passersby. Canal Park is also connected to Duluth's famous Lakewalk, a long boardwalk along Lake Superior, making it an easy starting point for a fine stroll in any season.

Minnesota Point is a long sandy peninsula that stretches for seven miles from Canal Park to the Superior Entry to the harbor.[2] It's home to Park Point Recreation Area, which boasts a sandy beach, a trail, ball fields and other amenities. The eastern end of the point is a prime spot for watching ships entering Superior's harbor.

The city of Duluth

Wisconsin Point is located in Superior, Wisconsin, and like Minnesota Point, it consists of a long sandy spit of land that runs parallel to the shore of Lake Superior.[3] With a sand beach that runs for two miles, the Superior Entry Lighthouse, and an abundance of trails and wildlife, the point is popular with locals and tourists alike. The western end of the point is also next to the entry for the Superior Harbor, making it a great place to watch ships enter and depart.

Ship Watching Hotline: (218) 722-6489

Tracking Ships Online: Visit ais.boatnerd.com or www.marinetraffic.com

Hidden Gems of Ship Watching: Skyline Parkway. For a bird's-eye view of the harbor and the city as a whole, take a trip along Skyline Parkway. Located high in Duluth's hills, the Skyline Parkway is 20-plus miles long and features over a dozen scenic overlooks, city parks, the Enger Tower (a five-story observation tower) and a bevy of trails.[4] Bring your binoculars—and a camera! For information, visit: www.skylineparkway.org.

Split Rock Lighthouse State Park is another famous site in the area to visit. Located in Two Harbors, Minnesota (about 30 miles from Duluth), the lighthouse was built after the infamous *Mataafa* Storm in 1905, which led to dozens of deaths and wrecked or damaged 20 vessels. Built on a massive cliff, all of the materials for the structure had to be hoisted up from the water as there were no roads or railroads in the vicinity. Once complete in 1910, the lighthouse operated until 1969.[5] Today, it has been restored to its previous glory and is now the site of a state park. The lighthouse beacon is lit once a year on November 10 to honor those lost in the sinking of the *Edmund Fitzgerald.*

Nearby: Located in Duluth, the *William A. Irvin* is a retired 600-foot ore boat that is now open for tours.[6] Berthed in Superior, the S.S. *Meteor* is the sole surviving whaleback-style ship on the Lakes. (A unique variety of design, the other whalebacks were either scrapped or were shipwrecked.) Today, the *Meteor* is a museum ship and is in the process of restoration, but it is open for tours.[7]

Addresses:

Canal Park: Canal Park Drive & Morse St

Minnesota Point: 45th St & Minnesota Ave

Wisconsin Point: Wisconsin Point Road, Superior, WI 54880

Split Rock Lighthouse State Park: 3713 Split Rock Lighthouse Road, Two Harbors, MN 55616

Contact Information:

Canal Park: Visit Duluth, (218) 722-4011

Minnesota Point: (218) 730-4300

Wisconsin Point: (715) 395-7270

Split Rock Lighthouse State Park: (218) 226-6372

Skyline Parkway: www.skylineparkway.org

William A. Irvin: www.decc.org/william-a-irvin/

S.S. *Meteor:* superiorpublicmuseums.org/s-s-meteor-2/

Aboard the *William A. Irvin* museum ship

The Soo Locks, Sault Ste. Marie, MI

What better place to ship watch than the key passage that enables ships to travel from Lake Superior to Lake Huron? During the shipping season, the Soo Locks are one of the premier ship watching destinations on the Lakes, as you can get up-close and personal with the ships at the Soo Locks Visitor Center.

Soo Locks Visitor Center: One of the best places to boat-watch on the Great Lakes, the Soo Locks Visitor Center has been a ship watching destination since ships began passing through the first locks in the 1850s. Open every day from Mothers Day until mid-October, the visitor center boasts an observation platform, exhibits, a theater, ship schedules and much more.[1] Every June the Soo Locks opens its doors on Engineers Day, a special treat for ship watchers, as it's the only day visitors can walk across the lock walls.

Ship Watching Hotline: Soo Locks Visitor Center, (906) 253-9290

Tracking Ships Online: Visit ais.boatnerd.com or www.marinetraffic.com

Hidden Gems of Ship Watching: The Soo Locks Boat Tours are a wonderful way to see the ships from a completely different perspective—from on the water. These tours allow you to travel alongside lake freighters and ocean-going vessels and to actually pass through the locks themselves. Dinner cruises and other special events are also offered.[2]

Another popular spot in Sault Ste. Marie is Clyde's, a drive-in restaurant located near the Sugar Island Ferry Docks. Both sites offer great views of the passing ships.[3]

The Soo Locks

Located about half an hour from Sault Ste. Marie, Dunbar Park is located along Lake Nicollet and isn't far from the West Neebish Channel, a man-made portion of the seaway that was blasted from rock. Known colloquially as "the rock cut," ships headed "downbound" (toward Lake Huron) must pass through this channel, making it a great place to boatwatch.[4]

Nearby: The Great Lakes Shipwreck Museum is based in Paradise, Michigan, about an hour from Sault Ste. Marie. Dedicated to the maritime history of the Great Lakes, the museum is especially well known for its exhibits and artifacts pertaining to shipwrecks on the Great Lakes. The museum famously houses the bell recovered from the ill-fated *Edmund Fitzgerald*, the huge ore boat that sank in 1975.[5]

And if you have a passport, Sault Ste. Marie, Ontario, is just across the St. Marys River!

Addresses:

The Soo Locks Visitor Center: 312 W. Portage Avenue, Sault Ste. Marie, MI 49783

Clyde's Drive-In: 1425 Riverside Dr, Sault Ste. Marie, MI 49783

Dunbar Park: 12878 S Scenic Dr, Sault Ste. Marie, MI 49783

Great Lakes Shipwreck Museum: 18335 N Whitefish Point Rd, Paradise, MI 49768

Contact Information:

The Soo Locks Visitor Center: www.lre.usace.army.mil/Missions/Recreation/SooLocksVisitorCenter.aspx; (906) 253-9290

The Soo Locks Boat Tours: www.soolocks.com

Clyde's Drive-In: (906) 632-2581

Great Lakes Shipwreck Museum: www.shipwreckmuseum.com; (906) 635-1742

Soo Locks Boat Tours: (800) 432-6301

An empty lock

Lake Michigan

St. Ignace, MI, and Mackinaw City, MI

Michigan's Lower Peninsula and the Upper Peninsula are separated by the Straits of Mackinac (pronounced *mack-in-naw*), a five-mile stretch of water that connects Lake Michigan and Lake Huron. Long an essential shipping corridor, the Straits are towered over by the massive Mackinac Bridge, which is five miles long with a main span of about 7000 feet and the only road to connect the Upper and Lower Peninsulas.[1] Often referred to as the "Mighty Mac," the bridge makes a spectacular backdrop for ship watching in the area and connects two great Michigan ship watching towns: Mackinaw City and St. Ignace.

Two ship passages approach the bridge: The busier Round Island Passage is a dredged channel located southeast of St. Ignace; found on Lake Huron, it skirts between Mackinac Island and Round Island before heading under the Mackinac Bridge and into Lake Michigan.[2] The South Channel approaches the bridge from the southeast of Mackinaw City, passing by Bois Blanc Island before reaching the bridge.

Mackinac Island State Park: Mackinac Island was the second national park to be established and the majority of the island has since become a Michigan state park. The park is famous for it stunning views, beautiful hotels and is perhaps most famous for its highway, M-185, which, like the rest of the island, doesn't allow automobiles. Instead horse-drawn carriage rides and bicycles are the primary modes of transportation.[3]

Located at the northern end of the Round Island Passage, the park is also a wonderful place to ship watch.

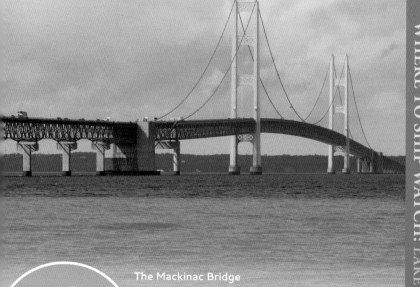

The Mackinac Bridge

The Mackinac Bridge: A vital transportation link, the Mackinac Bridge is a toll bridge with a per-car fee of $8. Unfortunately for ship watchers, walking across the bridge is only allowed twice a year (in spring and fall). Nonetheless, any mention of ship watching in the area would be incomplete without a mention of the bridge, as there's nothing like seeing a 1,000-foot ship dwarfed by the 8,000-foot bridge. Needless to say, a trip across the bridge is a must, and many businesses offer bridge tours on the water, making for great ship photo opportunities if the timing is right.[4]

Old Mackinac Point Lighthouse: Located on the south side of the Mackinac Bridge in Mackinaw City, the Old Mackinac Point Lighthouse was built in 1889 and operated for six decades. Tours of the lighthouse are available, and the site is also the home of the new Straits of Mackinac Shipwreck Museum, which features the many shipwrecks in this notoriously dangerous stretch of the Great Lakes.[5] All told, the area offers a lot to do, so whether you're taking photos of the bridge, the lighthouse or a passing freighter, there's more than enough maritime fun to keep you busy.

Straits of Mackinac Shipwreck Preserve: The Straits of Mackinac have been an important shipping corridor for hundreds of years, so it's not surprising that the area is home to many ship-wrecks. These shipwrecks are now part of the Straits of Mackinac Shipwreck Preserve, which is dedicated to commemorating and preserving the wrecks, which are diveable and often in very good condition.[6] Notable wrecks include the 600-foot *Cedarville*, lost in 1965, and the wooden brig *Sandusky*, lost in 1871.[7]

Tracking Ships Online: Visit ais.boatnerd.com or www.marinetraffic.com

Hidden Gems of Ship Watching: While there are many excellent places to ship watch in the area, one of the best is on Mackinac Island at the Fort Mackinac Tea Room.[8] The Tea Room overlooks the harbor, giving ship watchers a commanding view of the harbor and passing ships. Because ships will pass at a distance (roughly three-fourths of a mile), bring along your binoculars and zoom lens for the best view! Note: The Tea Room is open seasonally.

Nearby: The *Mackinaw* (hull number WLBB-30) is the Coast Guard's flagship on the Great Lakes, but it isn't the only Coast Guard vessel to have had that name[9]. It was preceded by another *Mackinaw*, known by its hull number of WAGB-83. Famous for its long service on the Lakes, "Mighty Mac" is now a museum ship that can be toured in Mackinaw City, Michigan.

Addresses:

Mackinac Island State Park: 7029 Huron Rd, Mackinac Island, MI 49757

Old Mackinac Point Lighthouse: 526 N Huron Ave, Mackinaw City, MI 49701

Contact Information:

Mackinac Island State Park: www.mackinacparks.com/parks–and–attractions/mackinac–island–state–park/

The Mackinac Bridge: www.mightymac.org

Old Mackinac Point Lighthouse: www.mackinacparks.com

Mackinac Tea Room: www.grandhotel.com/dining/fort-tea-room/

Straits of Mackinac Shipwreck Preserve: www.michiganpreserves.org/straits.htm

Mackinaw museum ship: www.themackinaw.org

The South Shore of Lake Michigan

From Chicago's Calumet River to northern Indiana, the southern shore of Lake Michigan is a destination for a variety of different kinds of vessels, including everything from bulk cargo carriers to river barges and container ships. Because of all this activity, the south shore is heavily industrialized, making it like something from a different world at times, but one well worth exploring.

The Calumet River: Much of the maritime cargo that enters Chicago heads to the Calumet River. The Calumet is lined with shipping terminals, railroad facilities and other transportation infrastructure (some active, some abandoned). Along the way, the river is crisscrossed with roads and bridges, some of which offer excellent views of passing ships. Given there are so many possible places to ship watch—there are seven crossings in the first six miles of the river—it's impossible to list them all.[1]

The East 92nd Street Bridge (listed as South Ewing Avenue Bridge on Google Maps) is one option, as is the 100th Street Bridge. Both have areas for pedestrians and offer a good vantage point to watch passing vessels. (Both are also drawbridges.) To give you an idea of where these bridges are, they are both within a mile of Calumet Park, which is located at 9801 S Ave G, Chicago, IL 60617.[2]

Port of Indiana, Burns Harbor: The south shore of Lake Michigan—especially northern Indiana—is a major center for steelmaking, which requires copious supplies of iron ore, coke and limestone; there are several massive steel mills in the area, including the ArcelorMittal mill at Burns Harbor. The Harbor also happens to be home to a public fishing pier operated by the Indiana Department of Natural Resources. To access it, you simply drive up to the security

The tall ship *Windy* in Chicago

checkpoint and tell the staff you're going to the fishing pier.[3] The pier is located at the end of the East Harbor arm and provides a good view of the incoming ships, especially vessels bound for ArcelorMittal's steel mill.

Indiana Dunes: There is another great ship watching option right next door to Burns Harbor: Indiana Dunes National Lakeshore. The shoreline stretches for 15 miles and is dominated by dunes and a sandy beach. The western end of the lakeshore runs right into the nearby steel plant, and you'll be able to get a pretty good look at ships coming and going from the harbor, as they are just under a mile away.[4]

Tracking Ships Online: Visit ais.boatnerd.com or www.marinetraffic.com

Hidden Gems of Ship Watching: The *Rouse Simmons* is one of the more famous ships in Chicago history. Known as the "Christmas Tree Ship," the *Simmons* was captained by Herman Schuenemann, who was famous for bringing Christmas trees directly from Michigan's Upper Peninsula and selling them from his ship in Chicago's harbor. The *Simmons*, which was often decked out in Christmas lights and had a Christmas tree on the mast, became a yearly tradition in the first decade of the twentieth century; unfortunately, it sank with all hands in a storm in 1912.[5] Today, the tradition continues, as the U.S. Coast Guard Cutter *Mackinaw* visits Chicago in early December to deliver Christmas trees, giving visitors a great chance to see the flagship of the U.S. Coast Guard fleet on the Great Lakes.

Nearby: The south shore of Lake Michigan is absolutely replete with things to do; examples include boat tours, a visit to Chicago's famous Navy Pier, and even tall ship festivals every few years.

A Safety Note: When you're ship watching, keep safety in mind. Many of the prime ship watching sites are in high-traffic areas (bridges, etc.) or areas where crime, private property and trespassing may be a concern.

Addresses:
The East 92nd Street Bridge and the 100th Street Bridge are both within a mile of Chicago's Calumet Park, which is located at 9801 S Ave G, Chicago, IL 60617. Be sure to check a map before you leave.

Burns Harbor is located at 6625 S Boundary Road, Portage, Indiana 46368

Indiana Dunes National Lakeshore: 1215 N. Indiana 49, Porter, IN 46304

Contact Information:

The Port of Burns Harbor:
www.portsofindiana.com/poi/burnsharbor/

Calumet Park:
www.chicagoparkdistrict.com/parks/Calumet-Park/

Indiana Dunes National Lakeshore: www.nps.gov/indu/index.htm

The Christmas Ship: christmasship.org

The U.S. Coast Guard cutter *Mackinaw* serving as the Christmas Ship

Lake Huron

DeTour Village

Located at the northwestern end of Lake Huron, DeTour Village is a charming town that parallels the DeTour Passage, a narrow corridor that connects Lake Huron to the St. Marys River and the Soo Locks some 50 miles later. Because the town is perched right next to the link connecting the lower four Great Lakes to Lake Superior, it's a perfect place to boatwatch and explore the area's maritime history.

DeTour State Dock: The Michigan Department of Natural Resources operates a public harbor in DeTour, complete with boat slips and a pier that stretches for 1,200 feet.[1] It gives good views of passing ships, but if you want an up-close look, be sure to bring your binoculars or a zoom lens for your camera.

DeTour Passage Historical Museum: Documenting the maritime history of the area, the DeTour Passage Historical Museum boasts maritime artifacts and displays, vintage photographs, and even the original Fresnel lens from the DeTour Reef Lighthouse.[2]

Drummond Island Ferry: The Drummond Island Car Ferry is the primary mode of transportation between DeTour Village and nearby Drummond Island.[3] It's also an experience that gives you a close-up look at the busy waterway, and if you're lucky, a passing freighter! Drummond Island is also worth exploring, as it offers hiking, boating, its own shipwrecks and a number of fine vantage points for ship watching.

Tracking Ships Online: Visit ais.boatnerd.com or www.marinetraffic.com

The view from DeTour Village
(photo by Cathy Kohring)

Hidden Gems of Ship Watching: To see DeTour Reef Lighthouse, you'll need to take a boat; it sits about seven-tenths of a mile off-shore, and about three miles (as the crow flies) from DeTour Village itself. Built in 1931, it remains an active aid to navigation and sits in 24 feet of water and rises 82 feet above the water. Tours of the structure are available seasonally by the DeTour Reef Lighthouse Preservation Society, which also offers a "Weekend Keepers" program, in which visitors can spend the weekend living on the lighthouse.[4] If you don't want to pay the tour fee of $75, you can also photograph the lighthouse from shore (though beware of private property), from a charter or from your own boat.

Nearby: Any area with a history of shipping will have shipwrecks, and DeTour is no different. There are over a dozen wrecks in the vicinity of DeTour Village, many of them accessible to divers, snorkelers, or even kayakers.[5] (A few are even visible from shore.) They are all now part of the DeTour Passage Underwater Preserve, which was established to preserve and protect the wrecks. The wrecks are impressive and range from nineteenth-century schooners to a construction crane that fell overboard in 2005.[6]

Addresses:

DeTour Village: 260 Superior St, DeTour Village, MI 49725

DeTour Passage Historical Museum, 104 Elizabeth Street, DeTour, MI, 49725

DeTour Marina: 600 Ontario St, DeTour Village, MI 49725

Contact Information:

DeTour Marina: (906) 297-5947

DeTour Village: www.detourvillage.com

Drummond Island: www.drummondislandchamber.com (this site also provides information for the Drummond Island Ferry)

DeTour Reef Light Preservation Society: drlps.com

DeTour Passage Underwater Preserve: www.michiganpreserves.org/detour.htm

The Drummond Island Ferry

Port Huron, MI

Port Huron is the gateway between the "upper" lakes of Superior, Michigan and Huron and the "lower" lakes, Erie and Ontario. This makes it an incredibly important shipping corridor, and one that is frequented by a veritable stream of different vessels, including everything from salties to 1000-footers. This makes it one of the premiere places to ship watch on the Great Lakes.

The Great Lakes Maritime Center at Vantage Point: The Great Lakes Maritime Center is located at the junction of the Black River and the St. Clair River, giving it a front-row view of the many ships that pass by. The Maritime Center is a must-see destination for any ship aficionado, as it features ship displays, well-known speakers and best of all, it's the home of the incomparable website Boatnerd (www.boatnerd.com).[1] Boatnerd.com is the go-to source for information about Great Lakes shipping; it's positively brimming with information, including everything from photo collections of the fleet and Great Lakes history to a yearly database listing all the saltwater vessels that have passed through the Great Lakes.[2] The brick-and-mortar home of Boatnerd features a real-time schedule of ship arrivals as well as a radio scanner, enabling you to know which ships will be in the vicinity and even allowing you to listen in on their radio transmissions.[3]

The Thomas Edison Parkway and the Blue Water Bridge: Just a quarter mile from Lake Huron, the Bluewater Bridge crosses the St. Clair River, connecting Michigan to the Canadian province of Ontario, which is just across the river. The U.S. side of the river is home to the Thomas Edison Parkway, which parallels the river and is a wonderful spot for ship watching.[4] (If you've got a passport, consider crossing the bridge to Sarnia, which is home to several parks, including Waterfront Park.)

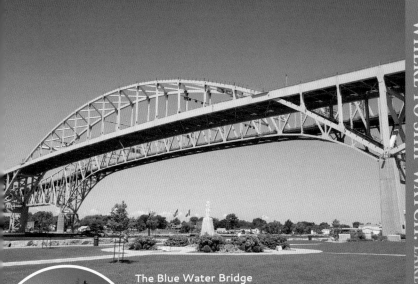

The Blue Water Bridge

Fort Gratiot Light Station: Found just north of the mouth of the St. Clair River, a light station has been in service in this area since 1825. The first lighthouse collapsed due to a poor design, but a new one was quickly built. The present lighthouse was built in 1829, and it is still in service.[5] At 82 feet high, it's an obvious presence on the shore and a popular spot for tours.[6] The charm and beauty of the lighthouse make it a wonderful backdrop for ship watching. Better yet, the nearby shoreline is quite busy, and ships pass within just a third of a mile.

Tracking Ships Online: Visit ais.boatnerd.com or www.marinetraffic.com

Hidden Gems of Ship Watching: One of the best ways to see the ships is from on the water! A number of companies operate day tours on the St. Clair River, and this is a great way to get a sense of just how large the ships of the Great Lakes really are. Tickets can be somewhat spendy ($20 per person), but the views are worth it.

Nearby: In the days before modern navigational equipment, lighthouses were essential tools to help mariners avoid danger. You can't build a lighthouse just anywhere, however; some dangerous reefs and shoals were simply unsuitable areas for construction of a lighthouse. That's where lightships came in. They served as floating lighthouses near dangerous areas, warning mariners to stay away. Lightship duty was incredibly perilous, as the ships had to weather even the worst storms. (Several lightships were lost in the line of duty early in the lightship service.) The last active lightship was the *Huron* (hull number LV-103); she served in southern Lake Huron until 1970.[7] Today the *Huron* is preserved as a museum ship and is now located in Pine Grove Park in Port Huron, where she can be toured for a fee. (Note: Closed-toe shoes are required on tours; tours are seasonal.)

Addresses:

The Great Lakes Maritime Center: 51 Water Street, Port Huron, MI 48060

Thomas Edison Parkway, just south of the Blue Water Bridge: 500 Thomas Edison Pkwy, Port Huron, MI 48060

Lighthouse Park and Fort Gratiot Light Station: 2802 Omar Street, Port Huron, MI 48060

Huron Lightship (located along the river near Pine Grove Park): 800 Prospect Place, Port Huron, MI 48060

Contact Information:

The Great Lakes Maritime Center: www.achesonventures.com/MaritimeCenter.aspx

Thomas Edison Parkway: porthuronrec.com/parks-beaches/

Lighthouse Park and Fort Gratiot Light Station: www.phmuseum.org/fort-gratiot-lighthouse/

Huron Lightship: www.phmuseum.org/huron-lightship/

The *Huron* Lightship Museum

Lake Erie

The Detroit Metropolitan Area

Once the manufacturing center of the U.S., Detroit's demographic troubles and crime issues are common knowledge; nonetheless, the city is still a vibrant center of culture and manufacturing, and it's also a great place to see passing ships in the Detroit River.

A safety note: Because of the above-mentioned struggles, when visiting Detroit it's prudent to be aware of your surroundings and to keep safety in mind. Always plan ahead before a visit, and take common-sense precautions.

Belle Isle State Park: Located on an island in the middle of the Detroit River, Belle Isle State Park is a great spot for ship watching, as ships pass right by the Island. You'll need a day pass ($9) to visit the island, but the trip gives you a number of great vantage points of passing vessels. (When you visit, head to the southern shore of the island, as the shipping channels are located just off shore.)[1, 2]

Bishop Park in Wyandotte, MI: Located about 15 miles from downtown Detroit, Wyandotte, Michigan, is home to Bishop Park, a park that parallels the Detroit River and gives ship watchers a fine view of the ships passing by. It's also home to a fishing pier, playground equipment and picnic shelters. Because the ships pass by the park in the middle of the shipping channel, be sure to bring binoculars or a telephoto camera lens for the best view.[3]

Tracking Ships Online: Visit ais.boatnerd.com or www.marinetraffic.com

The freighter *Saginaw* in Detroit

Hidden Gems of Ship Watching: While not a ship watching destination per se, a visit to the Detroit area is incomplete without a trip to The Henry Ford, which is located in nearby Dearborn, Michigan. Detroit's maritime history is intertwined with the history of the automobile industry in the area, and nowhere is that clearer than at The Henry Ford. The Ford Motor company didn't just build cars; it also made the steel that was used in the cars, mined the ore that went into the steel, and even owned a fleet of cargo freighters that transported the raw materials. At The Henry Ford you can see this history firsthand; you can even tour the famed Ford River Rouge Complex, the site where a good portion of the cargo carried by ore boats is put to use.[4] The observation deck at the plant offers a bird's-eye view of the area and is a great way to get perspective on just how tied the area is to industry.[5]

Note: The only downside to this visit is that admission is spendy at $18 per person; the River Rouge Tour is extra, at $15 per person. Don't let that dissuade you, however. The Henry Ford is widely considered one of the best tourist destinations in the region. It doesn't just cover the history of auto manufacturing; it is also home to a number of incredible exhibits, featuring everything from aviation and classic cars to Thomas Edison's reconstructed Menlo Park Laboratory and the chair in which Abraham Lincoln was sitting when he was shot. [6]

Nearby: Located on Belle Isle in Detroit, the Dossin Great Lakes Museum is dedicated to preserving the maritime history of the region.[7] The museum is home to a number of exhibits that will interest ship watchers, including the bow anchor of the ill-fated *Edmund Fitzgerald*, the elaborate Gothic Room of the S.S. *City of Detroit III* and the pilothouse of the S.S. *William Clay Ford*, an ore boat that visited Detroit on innumerable occasions.

Addresses:

The Henry Ford: 20900 Oakwood Boulevard, Dearborn, MI 48124-5029

Belle Isle State Park: East Jefferson and East Grand Blvd, Detroit, MI 48207

Bishop Park: (use Google maps) Wyandotte, MI 48192

The Dossin Great Lakes Museum: 100 Strand Drive, Belle Isle, Detroit, MI 48207

Contact Information:

The Henry Ford: www.thehenryford.org

Belle Isle State Park: 1-844-BELLE-PK (1-844-235-5375)

Bishop Park: www.wyandotte.net/departments/recreation/parks.asp

The Dossin Great Lakes Museum: detroithistorical.org/dossin-great-lakes-museum

The *Algoway* as seen from Belle Isle

Cleveland, OH

Like Detroit, Cleveland has long been a major manufacturing center. While the decline of the steel industry has hurt Cleveland, the Port of Cleveland is still a busy place and therefore a ship watching destination. Steel is still the dominant export from the port, which is often visited by lakers and salties alike. Lakers bring iron ore from further up the Lakes, and the salties generally load up with steel and carry it abroad. Cleveland's port is literally sandwiched between two large parks, making it a relatively easy place to ship watch as long as you keep an eye on the online ship-tracking websites.

Wendy Park and the old Coast Guard station: Just west of Cleveland's main port facilities, Wendy Park is situated in the middle of Cleveland's harbor. Better yet, it's also home to a pier that stretches into the harbor and leads to a (now-abandoned) Coast Guard station. This vantage point gives visitors a wonderful view of the harbor, and lake freighters can be seen on both sides of the pier. To the west, cargo freighters unload iron ore, where it is then deposited in rail cars. The mouth of the Cuyahoga River is to the east.[1] No longer the environmental nightmare it once was, the river remains a hub for shipping, so it's not uncommon to see ships entering the river or docking at the facilities of the Port of Cleveland just beyond the river mouth.

Whiskey Island Marina: Directly to the west of Wendy Park, the Whiskey Island Marina is another fine ship watching option. It's home to the Sunset Grille, a restaurant (open seasonally) with a good view that is often home to live bands in the summer.[2] (Better yet, the bar is situated in a refurbished sailboat.)[3]

A freighter in Cleveland

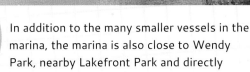

In addition to the many smaller vessels in the marina, the marina is also close to Wendy Park, nearby Lakefront Park and directly borders the Cleveland Bulk Terminal, where lake freighters often unload taconite and other materials. (The Cleveland Port and several other cargo facilities are also in the immediate area, making it possible to spot freighters, barges and other cargo vessels in several directions at times.)

Tracking Ships Online: Visit ais.boatnerd.com or www.marinetraffic.com

Hidden Gems of Ship Watching: Cleveland's lakefront is home to the Great Lakes Science Center, which now oversees one of the most famous vessels in Cleveland's history, the steamship *William G. Mather*.[4] An ore boat built in 1925, the *Mather* is 618 feet long and was in service on the Lakes until 1980. Intensively restored, the ship is now a museum ship that is open seasonally for tours ($8 admission fee per person), and it's the perfect side trip while ship watching.

Nearby: Located about half an hour from Downtown Cleveland, Cuyahoga Valley National Park gives visitors a look at the Ohio & Erie Canal and Towpath and the early days of shipping in the region. Built from 1825 to 1832, the canal was a 309-mile canal connecting Lake Erie to the Ohio River.[5] Once ships entered the canal, they were towed along by horses, which walked on a road that directly paralleled the canal. Abandoned after the rise of the railroads in the 1860s, some portions of the canal were later used as a water source, while other sections dried up. Today, Cuyahoga Valley National Park protects 20 miles of the canal, and features bridges, restored ship locks and the Canal Exploration Center, in addition to a wide variety of biking and hiking options.[6]

Addresses:

Wendy Park: To reach the park, take the Edgewater Park freeway ramp off Cleveland Memorial Shoreway (U.S. routes 6 and 20 and State Route 2). Getting to the park is a bit tricky, so be sure to look at a map before you leave.

Whiskey Island Marina: 2800 Whiskey Island Drive, Cleveland, OH 44102

Great Lakes Science Center: 601 Erieside Ave,
Cleveland, OH 44114

Cuyahoga Valley National Park: 1550 Boston Mills Road,
Peninsula, Ohio 44264

Contact Information:

Wendy Park: coastal.ohiodnr.gov/cuyahoga/wendypk

Whiskey Island Marina: www.whiskeyislandmarina.com/

Great Lakes Science Center: www.greatscience.com

Cuyahoga Valley National Park: www.nps.gov/cuva/index.htm

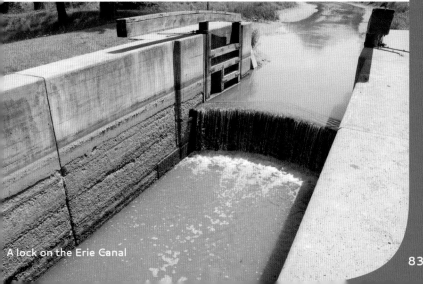

A lock on the Erie Canal

Lake Ontario

Northern New York: Eisenhower Lock Visitor Center

Ship watching on Lake Ontario in the U.S. isn't as easy as it is on the other Great lakes. Unless you can catch a ship coming into a Lake Ontario U.S. port, most of the "choke-points" of the St. Lawrence Seaway are in Canada, so you need a passport to view them. Unfortunately, most of the shipping channels on Lake Ontario are pretty far removed from shore, so even if a ship is passing by, you probably won't be able to see it. That doesn't mean folks on the lake are out of luck, however. On the contrary, the region of northwestern New York bordering the St. Lawrence is a great place to ship watch, as all ships heading to the Atlantic Ocean or venturing into the Great Lakes have to travel through the St. Lawrence Seaway. (And don't overlook Canada, either. See page 86 for some information about ship watching in Canada.)

Eisenhower Lock Visitor Center: The first U.S.-operated lock in the St. Lawrence Seaway, the Eisenhower Lock is one of the premiere spots to ship watch on the Great Lakes. Open from late June to early September (be sure to call ahead to confirm dates), the Visitor Center boasts a front-row view of the Eisenhower Lock, which enables ships up to 740 feet long to pass through. Over the course of a year, some 3,000 ships "lock through" the Eisenhower Lock.

Ship Watching Hotline: Eisenhower Lock Visitor Center: (315) 769-2422

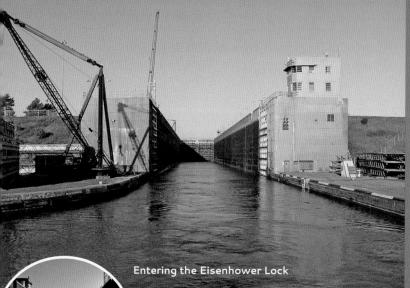

Entering the Eisenhower Lock

Tracking Ships Online: Visit ais.boatnerd.com or www.marinetraffic.com

Hidden Gems of Ship Watching: The St. Lawrence borders New York for more than 100 miles, so there are many different places to see ships. You'll need to do some exploring to find your favorite places to ship watch.

Addresses:

Barnhart Island Rd, Massena, NY (see website below for directions)

Contact Information:

www.seaway.dot.gov/explore/visitors-center

Canada: St. Catharines, Welland, Port Colborne and the Welland Canal

Now that a passport is required to enter Canada, a trip to Canada isn't as simple as a trip across the border. Nonetheless, it's still a great place to ship watch. Without question, the Welland Canal is one premiere ship watching destination.

Built to enable ships to bypass Niagara Falls, the first Welland Canal was built in the 1820s. Several iterations followed; the current canal (the fourth) was built from 1913 to 1932.[1] Spanning 27 miles in length, it's 26 feet deep and runs from St. Catharines in the north to Port Colborne in the south.[2] In between you can find the town of Welland; the canal once passed through the town and gives the canal its name, but the disruption caused by the ship traffic led to the construction of the Welland Bypass, a eight-mile-long channel that skirted downtown Welland. Like the canal itself, it was a monumental project, and one that took years to complete.

In all, the Welland Canals boast eight locks, as well as parks and bridge crossings, giving visitors many places to ship watch. One particularly good ship watching locale is the St. Catharines Museum and Welland Canals Centre.[4] Located in St. Catharines, Canada, right across from Lock 3 on the canal, the site features a museum dedicated to local history as well as a wonderful area to view the ships passing through the lock. A viewing platform is also available at Lock 7 in nearby Thorold, Ontario.[5] (Somewhat amazingly, most of the Welland Canal is drained each winter to make repair work possible.)

And when you're done ship watching, don't forget about a trip to the Canadian side of Niagara Falls!

An aerial view of the Welland Canal

Addresses:
St. Catharines Museum and Welland Canals Centre
1932 Welland Canals Parkway, St. Catharines, ON

Lock 7 Viewing Complex, Thorold: 50 Chapel Street South, Thorold, ON

Contact Information:
St. Catharines Museum and Welland Canals Centre:
niagarafallstourism.com/play/historic-sites/welland-canals-centre-lock-3/

Lock 7 Viewing Complex: (905) 680-9477

FLEETS ON THE LAKES

There are three primary freighter fleets on the Lakes at any time: a fleet of U.S.-flagged vessels, a fleet of their Canadian counterparts, and the combined fleet of the saltwater vessels that visit the Lakes. Learning about each fleet makes it easier to identify passing ships and helps ship watchers discern where they might be heading. Here is a general overview of each fleet as well as a closer look at a few specific vessels from each fleet on the Lakes.

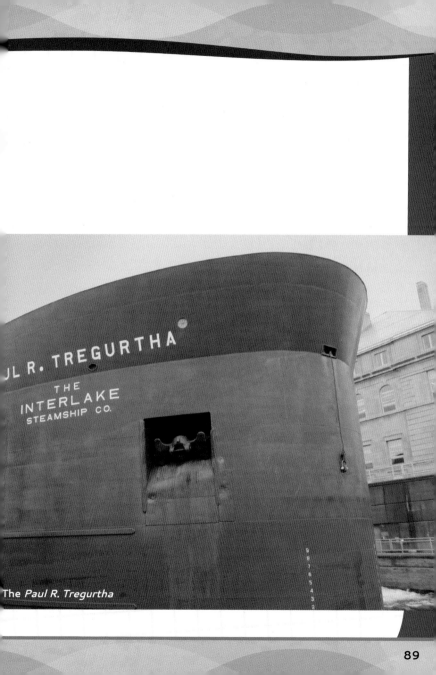

The *Paul R. Tregurtha*

The U.S. Laker Fleet

Newest: the tug-barge combination of the *Ken Boothe Sr.* and the *Lakes Contender*, built 2012[1]

Oldest: *Alpena*, built 1942[2]

Length: 487 feet to 1,013.5 feet[3]

Major Players: American Steamship Company, Grand River Navigation Company, Great Lakes Fleet, The Interlake Steamship Company, among several others

Capacity: Up to 71,000 tons (depending on the cargo)[4]

Primary Cargoes: iron ore, coal, limestone

The U.S. Great Lakes fleet consists of 57 vessels in all. With a few exceptions, there are two types of vessels in the U.S. fleet: self-unloading bulk carriers and tug-barge combinations.[5]

The U.S. fleet is arguably most famous for its 1000-footers, a series of 13 ships (including one tug-barge combination) that ply the waters of four of the Great Lakes. While only a fraction of the U.S. fleet consists of 1000-footers, most of the U.S. vessels on the Great Lakes are very large, much larger than those in the Canadian fleet. Because of their length, most are too long to pass through the Welland Canal to Lake Ontario. This means that much of the U.S. fleet is destined to remain on the four upper lakes. Even the vessels that could conceivably traverse the Lakes to the Atlantic Ocean are unlikely to do so.

When compared to the Canadian Fleet (see page 112), the ships of the U.S. Laker Fleet are older; nonetheless, age isn't necessarily a

The *Edgar B. Speer*

sign of a serious problem. As the freshwater of the Great Lakes isn't nearly as corrosive as saltwater, ship hulls last a great deal longer on the Lakes than they do on the high seas.[6] (One famous ship, the *St. Marys Challenger*, sailed on the Great Lakes for over one hundred years.)

The Canadian Laker Fleet has added quite a few new ships to its fleet over the past few years, but the U.S. fleet hasn't been standing pat. There have been a number of additions to the U.S. fleet; while a full-fledged new ship hasn't been built since the 1980s, a number of new tug–barge combinations have been built recently.[7] Given their economic benefits (they require fewer crew members) and versatility, this trend seems likely to continue.

About 1000-footers

Freighters that are 1,000 feet or longer

Number of 1000-footers on the Lakes: 13

Primary Cargoes: Iron ore, coal, limestone, grain, others

Capacity: From 58,000 to 78,850 tons[1]

Country of Registry: U.S.

Newest: The *Paul R. Tregurtha*, 1981.[2]

Oldest: The *Stewart J. Cort*, 1972[3]

Crew: 21–27, less for tug–barges

Length/Width: Up to 1,013 feet, six inches; 105 feet

Maximum Speed: Up to 15 knots

Ship Cost: Approximately $60 million in 1981 dollars[4]

Description: The largest vessels on the Great Lakes, there are 13 lake freighters over 1,000 feet in length. Because of their immense size, they are too large to pass through the Welland Canal on the St. Lawrence Seaway, so they are confined to a life on the "upper" four Great Lakes (Superior, Michigan, Huron, Erie). A 1000–footer can carry a staggering 70,000 tons of cargo, yet once they reach their destination, they don't need equipment or support from shore to unload, as they carry the equipment they need to unload aboard ship. Called self–unloading carriers, these ships feature a system of conveyor belts and booms that allow them to unload without the assistance of staff on shore. Thousand–footers can actually unload quite quickly—unloading thousands of tons of cargo per hour.

The *Paul R. Tregurtha*

The information on the 1000–footers listed below is listed in length and width in feet, and year built.

List of 1000-footers[5]

American Century
1,000, 105, 1981

American Integrity
1,000, 105, 1978

American Spirit
1,000, 105, 1978

Burns Harbor
1,000, 105, built 1980

Edgar B. Speer
1,004, 105, 1980

Edwin H. Gott
1,004, 105, 1978

Indiana Harbor
1,000, 105, 1979

James R. Barker
1,000, 105, 1976

Mesabi Miner
1,000, 105, 1977

Paul R. Tregurtha (Queen of the Lakes*) 1,013.5, 105, 1981

Presque Isle, (tug–barge unit)
1,004, 104.6, 1973

Stewart J. Cort
1,000, 105, 1972

Walter J. McCarthy Jr.
1,000, 105, 1977

*The longest ship on the Lakes is given the informal title of "Queen of the Lakes"

Laker Trivia
Mind-boggling statistics:
A 1000-footer can carry about 70,000 tons of freight, the equivalent of seven trains with one hundred cars each, or about 3,000 semi-trailers.[6]

Efficiency at its finest:
In terms of fuel efficiency required to move a ton of cargo, lakers are the most efficient mode of transportation out there, even besting railroads, which are hardly models of inefficiency.

A laker can move a ton of cargo over 600 miles on a gallon of diesel. Railroads can move a ton of freight 202 miles on a gallon of fuel.[7]

Bread for everyone!
A fully loaded laker holds 2 million bushels of wheat. Given that a bushel of wheat is enough to make 90 loaves of whole wheat bread, the wheat in one laker could make 180 million loaves of bread.[8]

The *Indiana Harbor*

The Paul R. Tregurtha

The largest vessel currently on the Lakes, the *Paul R. Tregurtha* is the current "Queen of the Lakes." She was launched in 1981 and originally was named the *William J. de Lancey* before being renamed in honor of Paul R. Tregurtha, the vice chairman of the board for the Interlake Steamship Company, which owns the *Tregurtha*. As company executives and customers were expected to travel aboard ship, no expense was spared when building the ship, and it features air conditioning, four swanky staterooms for guests, well-appointed crew quarters, elevators, and a dining room/lounge with an impressive view.[1] This earned her the nickname of the "Fancy DeLancey."[2]

Ship Specifications

Company: The Interlake Steamship Company

Based Out Of: Middleburg Heights, Ohio

Previous Names: William J. de Lancey (nicknamed the "Fancy DeLancey" because of its swanky accommodations)

Nickname: Big Paul

Entered Service: 1981[3]

Crew: 21–27

Length: 1013 feet, six inches[4]

Beam (width at widest point): 105 feet[5]

Capacity: 69,580 tons[6]

Fuel: Diesel

Maximum Speed: 13 knots[7]

Engine Horsepower: 17,120

Boom Length: 260 feet[8]

Hatches: 36[9]

Holds: 5[10]

Primary Cargoes: Primarily coal, sometimes iron ore

Unloading Rate: Can unload about 10,000 tons of ore per hour or about 6,000 tons of coal per hour

Ports Commonly Visited: Duluth, Detroit

Notable Accidents/Incidents: In August of 2012, the *Paul R. Tregurtha* was traveling on the St. Marys River when she ran aground.[11] The *Tregurtha* was about to enter the West Neebish Channel, the only route for downbound ships that leads from Lake Superior to Lake Huron. The channel, which is dredged to a depth of 28.5 feet, is over a mile long and was blasted directly from the rock when it was constructed, giving it the common name of The Rock Cut. Because of a navigational error, the *Tregurtha's* bow ran aground, and the current then swung the rest of the ship, grounding the stern as well. This blocked the entire channel, and the *Tregurtha* had to be re-floated and moved to allow shipping to continue. This took a day, and 13 ships had to wait to pass through the busy channel.[12] Thankfully, no one aboard the *Tregurtha* was hurt, though the ship did suffer some damage and was repaired shortly thereafter.[13]

The *Paul R. Tregurtha*

Indiana Harbor

Named in honor of the Great Lakes port of Indiana Harbor, it should be no surprise that the *Indiana Harbor* often visits her namesake port. She often heads there after loading iron ore from Minnesota's Iron Range or coal from the western U.S. The taconite is used at the sprawling steelmaking facilities in East Chicago, Indiana, which cover an astounding 3,100 acres—about 4.5 square miles.[1] The site is home to three blast furnaces and employs about 4,850 people.

The *Indiana Harbor* holds several Great Lakes shipping records; in 1993, she transported 71,369 net tons of coal on Lake Superior.[2]

Indiana Harbor also holds records for hauling the most coal upbound and downbound the Great Lakes.

Ship Specifications

Company: The American Steamship Company (Williamsville, NY)[2]

Entered Service: 1979

Nickname: The Big Indy

Crew: 21–27

Length: 1,000 feet[3]

Beam (width at widest point): 105 feet

Capacity: 80,900 tons[4]

Fuel: Diesel

Maximum Speed: 16 mph[5]

Engine Horsepower: 14,000[6]

Boom Length: 250 feet[7]

Hatches: 37[8]

Holds: 7[9]

Primary Cargoes: Iron ore, coal[10]

Unloading Rate: 10,000 tons per hour[11]

Ports Commonly Visited: Duluth, Indiana Harbor

Notable Accidents/Incidents: In 1993, the *Indiana Harbor* was involved in an accident that seems like something out of a one-liner: it hit a lighthouse. The Lansing Shoal Lighthouse sits about six miles offshore in northern Lake Michigan and serves as a warning for the Lansing Shoals, an area full of boulders and much shallower water than in the surrounding portions of the lake.[12] The *Indiana Harbor*, which had just left Sturgeon Bay, Wisconsin, was traveling at full speed when it grounded on the shoals, careening into the lighthouse in the process. The impact of the massive vessel gouged out a huge hole in the ship and also damaged the lighthouse, an impressive structure that sits upon a huge slab of concrete. Thankfully, the ship was able to return to port, and no one was hurt in the accident on the *Indiana Harbor* or the fully automated lighthouse. The Coast Guard investigation into the accident determined that the third mate, who was manning the ship, was negligent and failed to post a lookout.[13] When the ship ran aground, the captain quickly took command and freed the ship, which turned around and headed back to port for repairs.

The Presque Isle

One of the most unique ships on the lake, the *Presque Isle* actually consists of two parts—a tug and a barge.[1] Known as an integrated tug–barge, the tug fits into a notch on the stern of the barge and pushes the barge forward. While underway, the two components act as one ship; the tug and barge are not intended to separate while at sea. The integrated tug–barge was an attempt to lower crew costs and to improve on traditional barge service (which is very weather dependent), and there are now several other examples on the Great Lakes today. A more recent type of tugboat, called an articulated tug–barge, allows the tug some degree of movement on one axis, enabling greater efficiency and allowing the tug to operate separately, if necessary.

Ship Specifications

Company: The Great Lakes Fleet

Entered Service: 1973

Crew: 12–15

Length: 1,000 feet

Beam (width at widest point): 104.6 feet

Capacity: 57,500 tons[2]

Fuel: Diesel

Maximum Speed: 16 mph

Engine Horsepower: 15,000

Boom Length: 250 feet[3]

Hatches: 27[4]

Holds: 5[5]

Primary Cargoes: Coal, taconite

Unloading Rate: 11,200 tons per hour[6]

Notable Accidents/Incidents: In 2014, ice cover on the Great Lakes reached record levels.[7] Coast Guard icebreakers were busy breaking ice to make shipping possible, but despite their hard work, it led to a very slow start to the shipping season. When ships eventually were able to load cargo and start the season, they had to do so in convoys of ships led by Coast Guard icebreakers. This process took far longer than normal; ships on the Great Lakes usually travel at about 14 miles per hour or so, but the convoys practically limped along, and the ice damaged several ships. The *Presque Isle* was one of them, having to return to Two Harbors because of two small cracks in its hull. These were quickly repaired, and the ship was soon on the Great Lakes again.[8]

The *Presque Isle*

Arthur M. Anderson

At 767 feet long, the *Arthur M. Anderson* is not the largest ship operated by its parent company, the Great Lakes Fleet.[1] Nonetheless, the *Anderson* is undoubtedly one of the most famous ships in the Great Lakes fleet. In service since 1952, the Anderson is famous because of its connection to the *Edmund Fitzgerald*, the lake freighter that sank in a storm on November 10, 1975, taking its 29 crew members with her.[2] The *Arthur M. Anderson* was the last ship to see the *Fitzgerald* or communicate with her crew.

November 10, 1975

Both the *Anderson* and the *Fitzgerald* were transporting taconite on November 10, 1975.[3] The *Fitzgerald* left Superior, Wisconsin, at about 2:15 p.m. on November 9 and was headed to Detroit. The *Anderson* left Two Harbors at 4:30 p.m. on the same day and was traveling to Gary, Indiana. Given their similar destinations, they were headed along a similar course and only 10—20 miles apart, close enough to maintain visible contact with one another.[4] They knew a storm was forecast, as the National Weather Service had sent out warnings in advance. As the day progressed and headed into the 10th, the storm strengthened, and a full-fledged storm warning was announced. After consulting with one another, both captains decided to alter their course and avoid the traditional shipping lanes, in the hopes of avoiding some of the wind. This left them on a course that essentially headed out directly east across the lake. By the late afternoon of the 10th, the *Fitzgerald*, which was ahead of the *Anderson*, had taken some damage topside. In a radio call with the Captain of the *Anderson*, Captain McSorley of the *Fitzgerald* indicated he had a slight list and his pumps were running.[5] Later, he radioed in asking for navigational assistance, as both of his radar units were out; the *Fitzgerald* soon slowed its speed, in an attempt to let the *Anderson* catch up. The last radio conversation between the two ships took place at about 7:10 p.m. when the *Anderson* radioed the *Fitzgerald,* telling them about a ship approaching in the distance; as an aside, the *Anderson's* first mate asked how the *Fitzgerald* was doing; Captain McSorley responded, "We are holding our own."[6]

At that point, the storm was reaching its peak. Wind speeds have been estimated at 60—70 miles per hour, with gusts reaching hurricane force.[7] The waves the *Fitzgerald* encountered were almost certainly colossal. Average waves were an estimated 22 feet, and the storm may have produced much larger waves, perhaps up to 44 feet, taller than a four-story building.[8]

A few minutes after the last radio contact with the ship, the *Fitzgerald* was picked up on radar, but when the visibility cleared shortly thereafter, its lights were nowhere to be seen and the *Anderson's* crew couldn't find it on radar. The *Fitzgerald* was gone; after radioing the Coast Guard several times, the *Anderson* was able to sound the alarm about the missing ship. In the interim, she had made her way to relatively safer waters, but the Coast Guard soon asked the *Anderson* to turn around and head back into the storm to look for the *Fitzgerald*. Heroically, its crew did so, spearheading the search despite the awful weather. Over the course of the coming days, debris from the *Fitzgerald* and two empty lifeboats were discovered, but no survivors were found. The ship was eventually located in 530 feet of water.[9]

The *Anderson* has continued its service on the Great Lakes ever since.

The Canadian Great Lakes Fleet

Major Players: Algoma Central Corporation, Canada Steamship Lines, Coastal Transportation, International Marine Salvage, Groupe Desgagnés, Desgagnés Tankers, Lower Lakes Towing, McKeil Marine, Purvis Marine, among many others[1]

Length: Up to 740 feet long

Capacity: Up to about 38,000 tons

Primary Cargoes: Grain, iron ore, salt, slag, and many other products

The U.S. shares the Great Lakes with Canada, so the U.S. fleet is only half of the story when it comes to Great Lakes shipping. Actually, it's a bit less than that, as Canada's fleet is the largest on the Lakes. The entire U.S. fleet usually consists of around 56 vessels; for comparison, just three of the major Canadian players on the Great Lakes—the Algoma Corporation, Canada Steamship Lines and Groupe Desgagnés—have about 55 vessels between them.[2] In all, the total Canadian–flagged fleet tops 80 vessels, and several new vessels have recently entered service.[3, 4]

Canadian ships are somewhat different, however. While they are still massive—often 700 feet long—the Canadian ships are usually Seawaymax size (740 feet long or less), enabling them to travel on all of the Lakes and on the open ocean.[5] By comparison, the majority of the ships in the U.S. fleet were designed solely for use on the Lakes, which enables them to be much larger.

The *Algoma Quebecois*

Canadian ships also carry different goods. While the U.S. fleet is largely dedicated to iron ore and coal, the Canadian fleet ships a significant amount of grain (especially wheat and canola seeds) as well as salt, sand, gypsum, iron ore and coal.

John D. Leitch

The *John D. Leitch* is something of a throwback, as she was built with her pilothouse forward and the rest of the ship's quarters and accommodations to the rear. This style, which was quite common in the middle of the twentieth century, is rarer today, as most new ships are built with the pilothouse and other accommodations to the aft of the ship. Perhaps even more amazingly, she has only one cargo hold, which is massive.

Originally known as the *Canadian Century*, she was renamed in 2002 after she was retrofitted with a larger cargo hold.[1] Today, she is operated by the Algoma Corporation and carries bulk cargo, especially coal, from ports on Lake Erie to Canadian ports.

John D. Leitch

Company: Algoma Central Corporation[2]

Entered Service: 1967

Crew: 22[3]

Length: 730 feet[4]

Beam (width at widest point): 77 feet

Capacity: 20,031 tons[5]

Fuel: Diesel

Maximum Speed: 16 mph[6]

Engine Horsepower: 7,000

Boom Length: 256 feet

Hatches: 22

Holds: 1[7]

Common Cargoes: Primarily coal, but some other bulk cargoes

Unloading Rate: 4,500 tons per hour

Notable Accidents/Incidents: While the *John D. Leitch's* appearance draws a lot of attention for its fantastic design, it also briefly made headlines in 2012, when it collided with a 35-foot-long vessel operated by the Lorain County Sheriff's Department in Ohio.[8] The *Leitch* had taken on a load of coal and was winding its way through the Black River in order to reach Lake Erie on its way to Port Cartier in Quebec. It had just passed under a highway bridge and was heading north, only about a half mile from the open waters of Lake

Erie, when its stern got too close to the western shore, leading to a hydrodynamic effect called the "bank effect." This happens when close proximity to shore causes a vessel's bow to be pushed away from the shore (this is called a bow cushion). This causes a low-pressure area to develop toward a vessel's stern, causing it to be pulled toward the shore. This pushed the *Leitch's* bow toward the opposite shore, causing it to strike the law enforcement boat. Thankfully, no one was aboard the law enforcement boat, which sustained $500,000 in damage and later had to have its hull replaced.[9]

The *John D. Leitch*

OTHER SHIPS ON THE LAKES

Ships that ply the open oceans and visit the Great Lakes are known as salties. As you might expect, there are actually several kinds of "salty" ships; there are three types of salties: bulk cargo carriers, heavy lift ships, and chemical/fuel tankers. Bulk carriers often carry Lake Superior's more traditional cargoes (iron ore, coal, limestone and so on), whereas others arrive with shipping containers. Heavy lift ships feature large cranes and are ideal for transporting heavy cargo, such as wind turbine blades or other large equipment. Tankers transfer fuel or chemicals from site to site.

The *Zealand Beatrix*

About Salties

Types of Salties: Bulk cargo carriers, heavy lift ships, tankers[1]

Cargo capacity: Varies by vessel size, but averages around 20,000 tons[2]

Length: Varies; often from 320 to 650 feet[3]

Some of the Primary Shipping Companies: Wagenborg, Fednav, Eitzen, Navigation Maritime Bulgare, BBC Chartering, Flinter Shipping, Beluga Shipping[4]

Common Ports of Registry: The Netherlands, Cyprus, Liberia, China, Panama, Barbados, Antigua, among many others[5]

Age: Unlike vessels confined to the Great Lakes, saltwater vessels have a much shorter lifespan because their hulls corrode due to exposure to saltwater; this means that old salties are relatively rare. It's a generally safe bet that most salties visiting the Great Lakes were built in the last twenty years or so.

Description: Hailing from countries around the world, salties travel the open ocean and enter the Great Lakes Seaway system to engage in commerce. Because they aren't confined to the Lakes, salties aren't limited by geography. If you look up a saltie that visited the Great Lakes last summer, you might find that it's halfway around the world. This makes it impossible to predict if the ship you saw last summer will appear the following year. The only way to track down a specific saltie is to visit the many websites that track the AIS (automatic identification system)

A saltwater vessel near Duluth

data for commercial ships. Such sites (see page 174) will tell you where a ship is, where it has been and where it's headed.

While salties aren't limited by geography, size is a constraint. In order to travel through all five of the Great Lakes, they have to be small enough to fit through the St. Lawrence Seaway system, which means they have to be smaller than "Seawaymax"—740 feet in length. This means that the largest saltie on the Great Lakes will always be considerably smaller than the biggest laker. Nonetheless, this doesn't mean that the Great Lakes' 1000-footers are the longest ships in the world; on the contrary, some oil tankers have exceeded 1,500 feet in length.[6] Just as the 1000-footers on the Great Lakes are too large to leave the Lakes, those huge saltwater ships are simply too big to enter the Great Lakes.

Federal Elbe

A common visitor to the Great Lakes, the *Federal Elbe* is owned by
Fednav, a Canadian corporation that operates a large fleet of salties.[1]
While the ship is owned by a Canadian company, it flies the flag of
Cyprus. This practice, widespread in shipping, is called a "flag of
convenience." Companies opt to register in countries with fewer
regulations or lower fees in order to avoid the laws and fees of their
home country.

Federal Elbe

Length: 655 feet[2]

Port of Registry: Cyprus

Operated By: Fednav (Canada)

Beam (width at widest point): 77 feet[3]

Built: 2003[4]

Gross Tonnage: 22,654[5]

Maximum Speed: 14.5 knots[6]

Holds: 6[7]

Hatches: 6[8]

Cargo: Wheat, bentonite

About the Fednav Fleet: Based out of Montreal, Fednav ships are painted bright red, and their cranes and equipment are painted white, making them easily recognizable. The entire fleet boasts over 80 ships, many of which are dedicated to commerce on and through the Great Lakes.

Notable Accidents/Incidents: In 2006, the *Federal Elbe* was traveling from Montreal to Spain when a portion of its rudder broke, leaving the ship without the ability to steer in the middle of the ocean. The ship's cargo was offloaded and the ship was towed to Portugal, where repairs were made.[9]

Montreal, Fednav's home city

About Tugboats

Primary Cargoes: None

Oldest: The *Jill Marie*, operating since 1891[1]

Crew: Varies, but usually one to three

Maximum Length: Varies significantly; on the Great Lakes, tugs are often in the range of 30—90 feet

Horsepower: Around 1,000; newer models can have much more

Description: The unsung heroes of the Great Lakes, tugboats are commonly thought of as cute and diminutive, so much so that a tugboat was even the star of a popular children's show. Despite this impression, tugboats are actually fairly large vessels and incredibly powerful. Even though big lake freighters carry all the cargo, tugs are arguably the workhorses of the Great Lakes Fleet.

There are actually a number of different varieties of tugs.[2] Most are adapted for use in channels, rivers or harbors, where their power and maneuverability comes in handy, allowing them to guide the much more cumbersome lake freighters through narrow shipping passages and into berths. Other tugs are used to tow (or push) barges on rivers or the Great Lakes, or to remove sediment during dredging operations in a harbor.

Some tugs have been strengthened to serve as icebreakers during the long, cold winters of the north country, and some have even played important roles in rescues.

A tug breaking ice

This versatility has ensured that tugs have been a constant presence on the lake, and given their endurance—many are still in service after the better part of a century—that's not likely to change anytime soon.

Note: A couple of other types of tugboats are now found on the lake. Known as "integrated tugs" and "articulated tugs," these consist of a "tug" (essentially an engine and a pilothouse) that connects to the rest of a ship, which is basically a barge. These aren't traditional tugs, so I'm not including them here. See page 104 for a discussion of these tugs.

The Edna G.

One of the more famous tugboats on the Great Lakes, the *Edna G.* was built in 1896 and was a standard in Two Harbors, Minnesota, for the better part of a century.[1] Last used in 1981, she was the last steam-powered tugboat on the Great Lakes.[2] Originally built with a wooden hull, the *Edna G.* was initially dedicated to assisting ore boats. When she was later upgraded to a steel hull, she played an important role in a number of rescues.

The Edna G.

Built: 1896[3]

Length: 110[4]

Beam (width at widest point): 23 feet[5]

Horsepower: 1,000[6]

Fuel: Coal

Description: The *Edna G.* was designated as a National Historic Site in 1974, and she is a local landmark in Two Harbors. Efforts are underway to preserve her for the future, but her status is uncertain, as maintaining a vessel of her age is expensive and time-consuming. To get involved, visit friendsofednag.org.

Believe it or Not: Just how old is the *Edna G.*? At one point, she was confiscated by the government to join the war effort. The war effort in World War I, that is.

Notable Rescues: While the *Edna G.* spent most of her time working with ore boats, she was also used as a "fire tug" (a fire-suppression ship).[7] She also played a role in rescuing the crew of the *Madeira* during the infamous *Mataafa* Storm of 1905.[8] Considered one of the worst storms in Lake Superior history, the storm led to 29 shipwrecks and 33 deaths. The storm is named for the *Mataafa*, which split into three parts trying to re-enter Duluth's harbor, killing the nine members of its crew who were stranded in the aft portion of the ship. Because of the storm, rescue crews couldn't reach them, and the nine crew members died of exposure.

The *Edna G.* was active in rescuing crew members of the *Madeira*, another vessel sunk in that storm. The *Madeira* was being towed by the *Edenborn*.[9] The *Edenborn* cut the ship loose, hoping the *Madeira* could set anchor and ride the storm out. Instead, the *Madeira* was driven on the rocks and pushed against a sheer rock cliff. One of the crew members was somehow able to climb the 60-foot cliff and was able to use a rope to rescue all of the crew, except for one, who was drowned when the *Madeira* finally went under. As news of the storm got out, tugboats and other vessels were sent to search for missing vessels, and the *Edna G.* was sent to look for the *Madeira*. She located the missing crew two days later, taking them aboard and recovering the body of the crew member who drowned.[10] The storm led directly to the construction of Split Rock Lighthouse located near Two Harbors, MN.

Aboard the *Edna G.*

About the Coast Guard

Total Ships: 10 cutters, with four different classes of cutters; many aircraft and smaller vessels

Newest Ship: The *Mackinaw*, commissioned 2006

Oldest: The *Buckthorn*, commissioned 1963

Maximum Length: 240 feet, *Mackinaw*

Minimum Length: 100 feet, the *Buckthorn*

Description: The U.S. Coast Guard's Ninth District operates 10 ships on the Great Lakes. Referred to as "cutters," each of these ships exceeds 65 feet in length and has facilities for a crew to live onboard. In all, there are four classes of Coast Guard ships currently on the Lakes; they range in size from the 100-foot *Buckthorn* to the 240-foot *Mackinaw*.[1]

The Coast Guard Fleet on the Great Lakes[2]

Seagoing Buoy Tender/ Icebreaker (240 feet)
Mackinaw (Homeport: Cheboygan, MI)

Juniper-Class Seagoing Buoy Tender (225 feet long)
Hollyhock (Homeport: Port Huron, MI)
Alder (Homeport: Duluth, MN)

Bay-Class Icebreaking Tug (140 feet)
Biscayne Bay (Homeport: St. Ignace, MI)
Bristol Bay (Homeport: Detroit, MI)
Katmai Bay (Homeport: Sault St. Marie, MI)
Mobile Bay (Homeport: Sturgeon Bay, MI)

The U.S. Coast Guard cutter *Biscayne Bay*

Morro Bay (Homeport: Cleveland, OH)
Neah Bay (Homeport: Cleveland, OH)

Inland Buoy Tender (100 feet long)

Buckthorn (Homeport: Sault St. Marie)

History: The U.S. Coast Guard has been active on the Great Lakes almost as long as commercial shipping has existed on the Lakes, but it hasn't always been called the Coast Guard.[3] In fact, what we know today as the Coast Guard originally consisted of four different federal organizations: The U.S. Lighthouse Service, the Revenue Cutter Service, the Life–Saving Service, and the more obscure Steamboat Inspection Service.

The Lighthouse Service was responsible for establishing and maintaining and supplying lighthouses; it also maintained a fleet of light ships, ships that remained anchored in areas where lighthouses couldn't be built. (Other ships, called lighthouse tenders, would resupply lighthouses and light ships.) All of these tasks were monotonous, difficult, and occasionally dangerous jobs. They were also very important; prior to the advent of GPS, radar and radio, lighthouses were a crucial navigational tool.

The Revenue Cutter Service patrolled the Great Lakes, enforcing U.S. law, combating smuggling and occasionally even chasing down timber pirates and other criminals.

The Life–Saving Service had an obvious job; it established life–saving stations crewed with "surfmen" who aided ships, swimmers and sailors in distress. Like the rescue swimmers of today's Coast Guard, the work of the Life–Saving Service crews was incredibly dangerous, especially since reliable motorized rescue boats simply didn't exist until well into the Life–Saving Service's history.[4] This meant that the Life–Saving Service often had to row or sail into the storms that caused the (often powered) vessels to founder or run aground.

The Steamboat Inspection Service was the least heralded of the Coast Guard progenitors, but it played an important role. Steam-boats were powered by powerful engines, but they could easily cause fires or even explode if improperly maintained. (That's exactly what happened when the *Sultana* exploded on the Mississippi, then sank, killing an astounding 1,800 people, more than were lost with the *Titanic*.)[5]

By an Act of Congress, the Life–Saving Service and the Revenue Service were combined in 1915 to create the Coast Guard.[6] By the mid–1940s, all four of the aforementioned services were subsumed by the Coast Guard. Over the course of its 200-year history, the Coast Guard is estimated to have saved up to a million lives.

Not Just Search and Rescue

As a branch of the Armed Forces, the Coast Guard has also served in every major military conflict in American History, with many members serving in combat. Coast Guard crews even sunk an estimated 11 German submarines (some just off the U.S. coast) in World War II.[7] Over the last 60 years, 582 Coast Guard members have died in combat.[8]

Armed Vessels on the Great Lakes

The Coast Guard has been active with military ships on the Great Lakes, too. During Prohibition, the Coast Guard was engaged in the "Rum War" against rum runners smuggling rum in from Canada on the Lakes (and on the Atlantic Coast).[9] On the East and West coasts, the Coast Guard adapted a fleet of former Navy Destroyers and 75-foot picket boats to combat rum running. A fleet of 25 of these picket boats was also dispatched to the Great Lakes, patrolling until 1928. They were armed with a .30 caliber machine gun and a one-pounder machine gun.[10]

The USCGC Mackinaw

U. S. COAST GUARD

The successor to the famed *Mackinaw*, the first heavy icebreaker on the Great Lakes (which is now a museum ship), this is the second Coast Guard cutter to be known as the *Mackinaw*. Like her forbearer, one of the *Mackinaw's* primary duties is heavy icebreaking, an incredibly important task for the shipping industry, as icebreaking significantly expands the shipping season on the Great Lakes and is required during roughly one-quarter of the season. Icebreaking (and freeing vessels stuck in ice) has serious economic benefits, estimated to be worth tens of millions of dollars each year.[1]

The *Mackinaw's* other duties include buoy tending, law enforcement activities, environmental clean-up and search-and-rescue operations. A high-tech ship, the Mackinaw is well equipped for any contingency; an automated computer system allows it to maintain its position, even amid rough seas.

The USCGC Mackinaw

Built: 2006[2]

Crew: 55[3]

Length: 240 feet[4]

Maximum Speed: 15 knots[5]

Horsepower: 4,460[6]

Ship Cost: $80 million

Homeport: Cheboygan, MI

Notable Events and Rescues: The *Mackinaw* and the Coast Guard's other ships are incredibly important as icebreakers, especially during severe winters. The bitter winter of 2014 proved just how important the *Mackinaw* is to Great Lakes shipping, as she spent much of the spring leading convoys of lake freighters through the ice. The ice season was so bad that steel mills and factories on the lower lakes had to scale back production because of a lack of raw materials. These convoys continued well into April; making the *Mackinaw* and the other Coast Guard cutters the star players of the spring shipping season.

A common fixture at public events and ports throughout the Great Lakes, the *Mackinaw* is one of the most well-known vessels on the Great Lakes and one of the public faces of the Coast Guard. It's also surprisingly accessible; visitors can tour the *Mackinaw* and other Coast Guard ships at the Grand Haven Coast Guard Festival, which is held in Grand Haven, Michigan, every summer.[7]

The Mackinaw also plays a regular role in rescues on the lake. Her crew responded to a storm that struck many of the vessels in the famous Chicago to Mackinac Island sailboat race.[8] The *Mackinaw* was serving as the escort of the race when a storm hit with gusts of up to 67 knots, knocking down 37 ships in all. A 35-foot boat named the *WingNuts* was taking part in the race and capsized, sending six of its crew of eight into the water. Two of the crew members were trapped under the boat and drowned; they apparently suffered head injuries shortly after the accident.[9] The survivors huddled on the hull of the overturned boat, and two of them activated emergency response devices. The crew was able to attract the attention of a nearby vessel, the *Sociable*, which rescued the six survivors and communicated with the Coast Guard. A 41-foot Coast Guard vessel from Charlevoix, Michigan, arrived, followed by a Coast Guard helicopter. The *Mackinaw* arrived about five hours after the accident and became the command center.[10] (As the *Mackinaw* was some distance away, it couldn't respond immediately.) An analysis of the accident concluded that the *WingNuts* capsized because it was too unstable and unsuitable for use in a long-distance race.

The U.S. Coast Guard Cutter *Mackinaw*

About Tall Ships

While sailing vessels have long since been supplanted by powered vessels, sailing ships can still be seen on the Great Lakes. Known as "tall ships" because of the impressive height of their masts, tall ships are traditional sailing vessels, and they come in a variety of forms, from 200–foot–long fully rigged ships with three (or even four) masts to the much smaller sloop, which only has one mast. No matter what size the ships are, they are an impressive sight to see.

Tall Ships Festivals: If the sight of one tall ship is thrilling, imagine seeing a handful! Thanks to tall ships festivals, you can. Such festivals feature tall ships from around the world and usually occur every few summers on the Great Lakes.[1] The ships make their way from one Great Lakes port to another, drawing huge crowds at each one.

Ports visited during the last festivals included: Duluth, MN, Sault Ste. Marie, WI, Green Bay, WI, Chicago, IL, Bay City, MI, Cleveland, OH, Erie, PA, as well as a host of Canadian Ports (including Toronto).[2]

When the large ships aren't on the Lakes, they are usually touring elsewhere, including the Atlantic or Pacific Coast, so be sure to check the tall ships website for more information (www.sailtraining.org/).

Other sailing vessels stay on the Lakes. Just a few examples include:

The *Brig Niagara* (Erie, Pennsylvania)
The *Manitou* (Traverse City, MI), which even operates a floating bed and breakfast

The *Brig Niagara*

The *Nauti-Cat* (Traverse City, MI)

The *Madeline* and several others (Traverse City, MI)

The *Hjørdis* (Grand Marais, MN)

The *Friends Good Will* (Grand Haven, MI)

The *Kajama* (Toronto, Canada)

The *Windy* (Chicago, IL)

The *Red Witch* (Chicago, IL)

The *Appledore IV* (Bay City, MI)

The *Liberty* (western New York)

See page 174 for web links.

The Bounty

The original H.M.S. *Bounty* was a British vessel that was the site of an infamous mutiny in 1789.[1] This re-creation, built in 1960, was created for use in the 1962 film *Mutiny on the Bounty,* which starred Marlon Brando. Built larger than the original ship in order to accommodate filming equipment, the ship was a fully fledged sailing vessel and was sailed to its shooting locations, some of them in the South Pacific.

After the film was completed, the ship was sold several times, including to Ted Turner (when he acquired MGM). After that, it was donated and soon became somewhat dilapidated. Then, it was purchased by another organization—the HMS Bounty Organization, LLC, which took the ship on tours.

The Bounty

Built: 1960[2]

Crew: 16[3]

Type of Ship: Fully rigged tall ship

Length: 180 feet[4]

Speed: 6 knots

Ship Cost: $4 million

The Sinking of the *Bounty*: Because wooden vessels are inherently more fragile than steel ships, their captains tend to avoid serious weather if possible. This is especially true when it comes to hurricanes. Unfortunately, when Superstorm Sandy was approaching the East Coast in 2012, the *Bounty's* captain decided to set sail for Florida, in the hopes that he could outrace the storm. (The ship had engines in addition to sails.) Needless to say, this was an incredibly irresponsible decision, especially for a ship with a relatively inexperienced crew, no real engineer, and given the fact that the vessel was known to be prone to leaking in normal conditions. For the first day or so, the ship headed southeast and didn't encounter the storm; the captain then inexplicably decided to head southwest, cutting in front of the storm. This proved to be a fatal error, as the slow *Bounty* took an absolute pounding amid 20–30 foot seas and 90-knot winds.[5] This caused it to take on more water, eventually leading its generators, engines and pumps to fail. This effectively left it dead in the water; the crew then contacted the Coast Guard, which sent a C-130 aircraft to maintain communication. The captain still refused to issue an order to abandon ship, and the crew didn't leave the vessel until it was rocked by a large wave and the crew was literally thrown into the water. Unfortunately, a crew member and the captain died in the incident, and several others were seriously injured, and the *Bounty* is now at the bottom of the Atlantic.[6]

The shipwreck of the *Bounty*

SHIPWRECKS AND ACCIDENTS

Thanks to improved safety standards and navigational and communication equipment, shipwrecks are far less common today than even fifty years ago. Unfortunately, sailors on the Great Lakes weren't always so lucky. The Great Lakes Shipwreck Museum estimates that 30,000 sailors have died in the 6,000 recorded shipwrecks on the Lakes.[1] If anything, that count is almost certainly conservative, as some historians estimate there may have been 25,000 wrecks in all.[2] These wrecks were the result of many factors: human error, uncharted waters, mechanical failures, and of course, the unforgiving gales of November.

From the infamous shipwreck of the *Edmund Fitzgerald* to the loss of older vessels like *Le Griffon*, the shipwrecks of the Great Lakes tell a tale that is equal parts history, tragedy and adventure. The following is just a sampling of the many wrecks on the Great Lakes.

The *Paul R. Tregurtha*

The First Recorded Shipwrecks on the Great Lakes

Frontenac and Le Griffon

Shipwrecks have undoubtedly occurred on the Great Lakes for thousands of years, but the first shipwrecks in the Great Lakes historical record are tied to the famous French explorer Rene–Robert Cavelier, Sieur de La Salle. La Salle was among the most prominent French explorers on the Great Lakes. In the course of searching for the fabled Northwest Passage, La Salle built a pair of ships to take advantage of the local fur trade. The first reputed vessel on the Lakes, the *Frontenac* was a small vessel and was wrecked near Thirty Mile Point on Lake Ontario.[3] A second much larger vessel was soon built to replace it; named *Le Griffon*, it was finished in a hurry, as the French explorers feared an attack by the native Iroquois.[4] After

successfully traveling to Lake Michigan, the ship landed at Washington Harbor; afterwards, La Salle ordered it sent back to Niagara loaded with furs in order to settle his expedition's debts. Six men were aboard when it set off; the ship was never heard from again, and it likely sank in a storm or struck the nearby shoals which the American Indians had warned the explorers about. Considered among the most important shipwrecks in Great Lakes history, the ship is arguably the "Holy Grail" of shipwrecks because of its historic value and is now the subject of a dedicated search.[5]

The War of 1812 on the Great Lakes

The *Scourge* and the *Hamilton*

Not all ships that have sunk on the Great Lakes have been commercial vessels; given that control of the Great Lakes was contested through much of recent history, naval vessels have also plied the waters of the Lakes. Several of these vessels went down; the *Scourge* and the *Hamilton* are two famous examples.[6] Merchant ships that were conscripted into the U.S. Navy, the two vessels went down after capsizing in a storm on Lake Ontario in 1813.[7] The wrecks, which were discovered in 1973, were remarkably intact in 290 feet of water.[8] The finds include both figureheads on the front of the vessels, cannons, cannonballs, and even entire skeletons. As they are literally watery graves, they are designated as protected sites; diving on them is now punishable by a very large fine. Unfortunately, the wrecks are now effectively covered by invasive zebra mussels.

H.M.S. *Speedy*

The U.S. Navy wasn't the only one to lose a ship on the Great Lakes. The Royal Navy lost the H.M.S. *Speedy* on Lake Ontario in 1804.[9] The ship, which was traveling from the city of York (present-day

Toronto) to Newcastle (now Presqu'ile Provincial Park) to transfer a prisoner for a trial, sunk after striking a reef during a storm.[10] Despite its name, the *Speedy* was actually a slow ship, and given its leaks and condition, she had no business being on the lake. The captain had protested, but he was overruled because of the importance of the trial and the ship's cargo—six copies of the new Constitution for Upper Canada. The captain was also aware of the reef in the area and tried to avoid it, but unbeknownst to him his compass reading was off significantly because of magnetic anomalies in the area. Once it hit the rocks, the ship quickly went down. Her wreck may have been discovered by wreck diver Ed Burtt, but because of Canadian federal regulations, artifacts can't be removed until a government-funded public display site is found. Unfortunately, Burtt has been waiting for more than two decades.[11]

Treasure Ships? Well, There Was One: The S.S. *Comet*

Most of the cargoes on the Great Lakes are pretty pedestrian: iron ore, grain, coal and timber, so almost no ships went down with doubloons or jewels or treasure. One, however, did: The S.S. *Comet* was carrying 70 tons of silver ore from Montana when she sank after being inadvertently rammed in 1875.[12] The ship now lies in 230 feet of water in Whitefish Bay on Lake Superior and its remains are almost perfectly preserved. The silver ore, however, has been dashed across the lake bottom.

The *Mataafa*

The infamous *Mataafa* Storm of 1905 is considered one of the worst storms in Great Lakes history. The storm packed winds of 60 miles per hour and struck Lake Superior especially hard, leading to 29 wrecks and 33 fatalities.[13] A good portion of the fatalities occurred on

FATE OF STORM-RACKED BOATS THE SECRET OF LAKE SUPERIOR

WRECK OF THE STEAMER MATAAFA.
Nine Men Perished on This Vessel, Which Was Wrecked Near the Entrance to the Duluth Ship Canal—Fifteen Who Took Refuge in the Captain's Cabin, Forward, Were Rescued After a Night of Torture.

the *Mataafa*, which was towing a barge. A day after leaving the harbor, the weather deteriorated and the captain decided to turn back to port. When the ship approached Duluth harbor, the captain decided to jettison the towed vessel and attempt to bring the *Mataafa* into the safety of the port. Unfortunately, just as the ship entered the canal, a rush of water pushed the ship into the harbor wall, eventually flinging it back into the lake, where it collided with the pier. The ship soon split into three pieces, stranding sailors at both ends of the ship. Even though the ship was only a matter of feet from safety, the horrified onlookers could do nothing. Rescuers saved the crew from the front of the ship, but the nine men stuck at the rear of the ship died; in some cases, their bodies had to be chipped from ice.[14]

The *Madeira*

Unlike the *Mataafa*, which was a powered vessel, the *Madeira* was a barge, but she was stuck in the same storm. Being towed by the steamer *Edenborn*, the *Madeira* was cut loose, as the captain of the *Edenborn* hoped the *Madeira* would be safer riding out the storm on her own. Unfortunately, the *Madeira* was instead pushed against Gold Rock—a 60-foot cliff—where the ship took an absolute beating.[15] Meanwhile, the *Edenborn* was driven ashore, where it split into two; one crew member died. Amazingly, most of the *Madeira* crew survived, thanks to crew member Fred Benson, who jumped onto a ledge, scaled the rock wall and managed to hoist his crew mates up with a rope. Only one crew member perished; he died as the ship collapsed around him as he tried to climb to safety.[16]

The Loss of the *Rouse Simmons* and Captain Santa

The loss of the *Rouse Simmons* is among the strangest shipwrecks in Great Lakes history. The vessel's captain was Herman Schuenemann, a merchant who first transported lumber; he soon realized that if he cut out the middleman, he could transport Christmas trees directly from Michigan to customers in Chicago. The tactic worked, and such Christmas ships became popular. Schuenemann and his ship quickly became a regular fixture in Chicago during the Christmas season. His ship, strung up with lights, was known informally as "the Christmas Ship" and Schuenemann was known as "Captain Santa."[17] Unfortunately, the relatively small vessels were sailing at the very end of the sailing season—November—when the worst storms occurred. An old, creaky vessel, *Rouse Simmons* was no match for the storm that struck Lake Michigan on November 12, 1912.[18] Once the storm's strength became clear, it was apparent the ship was in trouble. Two Life-Saving Stations reported seeing the *Simmons* signaling for distress, and one sent a motorboat to assist her, but by the time it got there, it was too late; the ship and her crew were never seen again. That is, until the ship's wreck was located in the 1970s; a Christmas tree was brought to the surface from the wreck and is now on display at the Port Washington Light Station.[19]

The French Minesweepers *Inkerman* and *Cerisoles*

Both built in 1918, the *Inkerman* and the *Cerisoles* were two newly constructed French minesweepers headed out from Thunder Bay with the eventual destination of France.[20] The ships were never heard from again, which is especially strange given that they were modern ships equipped with radio. In all, 78 sailors died; it was the worst ship-wreck on the Great Lakes proper; the *Eastland* Disaster, which occurred on the Chicago River when a cruise vessel capsized, killed a staggering 800 people and is far and away the largest disaster in Great Lakes history.[21]

The *Daniel J. Morrell*

The *Daniel J. Morrell*

A 586-foot bulk freighter, the *Daniel J. Morrell* sank in Lake Huron in a storm on November 29, 1966.[22] The ship encountered winds of 65 miles per hour and waves of 30 feet. As the Coast Guard later confirmed, the ship was built with a type of steel popular in ship-building prior to 1948; this steel exhibited brittleness when exposed to temperatures below 50 degrees, compromising its structural integrity.[23] The sole surviving crew member, Dennis Hale, lived to tell what happened. He was off-duty in his cabin toward the front of the ship when he heard a series of loud noises, and he noticed the power was out. He immediately went on deck and he couldn't see the stern of the ship. This happened because the center of the ship was rising above the ends of the ship; this is called hogging and it occurs when a ship's hull undergoes enough stress to bend and eventually break. The stern rose back up, but by this point, the ship was doomed; the crew, including the only survivor, were gathered in the front portion of the ship around a life raft and simply had to watch as the two portions of the ship separated.[24] Amazingly, the rear portion of the ship still had power and the engine was still going. This caused the two sections to smash together, causing a great deal of sparks; eventually the front portion of the ship was bent perpendicular to the aft section. The crew couldn't do much else than wait for the ship to sink. Worse yet, as it was the middle of the night (2 a.m.), they were ill-prepared for a trip into the cold waters of Lake Huron; while four crew members managed to get to the life raft, there was only one survivor. The crew member who survived was only wearing his underwear and a great coat; he couldn't find his pants in the darkness.

Rescue crews weren't dispatched until ten hours later, when the *Daniel J. Morrell* was reported overdue by the shipping company, forcing the survivors to weather the storm all night without any way to stay warm. When help eventually arrived 14 hours later, three of the crew members had died, one just before the Coast Guard arrived. (Today, the Coast Guard aims for a two-hour response time.)[25] The survivor lived to tell the tale, and has since authored a well-received account of his survival.[26]

The *Edmund Fitzgerald*

The most famous shipwreck in Great Lakes history, the *Edmund Fitzgerald,* went down in Lake Superior in a major storm on November 10, 1975. The 729-foot ore freighter sank with her crew of 29 aboard, and her loss was a complete shock to the Great Lakes community. She was a modern vessel, with high-tech navigational and communications equipment, and she wasn't alone in the storm: another Great Lakes freighter, the *Arthur M. Anderson* (see page 108), was in communication with her throughout the storm, and was even attempting to catch up to the *Fitzgerald*. Captain McSorley of the *Fitzgerald* reported to the *Anderson's* crew that the *Fitzgerald* had a list and had its

pumps running, but when prompted later about their status, Captain McSorley of the *Fitzgerald* replied, "We are holding our own."[27]

The ship was never heard from again, and it soon disappeared from radar. There are many possible theories about the *Fitzgerald's* sinking: the Coast

Guard investigation maintained that the hatch covers were not sufficiently sealed, allowing the ship to take on water in its cargo hold. Others disagreed. Some suggest the ship got too close to shallow water and "shoaled," causing hull damage, or that the ship's hull suffered a stress fracture and broke up on the surface. A more recent theory is that the ship was struck by a rogue wave; once considered sailors' tales, rogue waves are now a documented phenomenon on the open oceans, and it's likely they have occurred on the Great Lakes as well.

Whatever the cause, weather played a major role. According to one analysis of the weather conditions on the night of the accident, the *Fitzgerald* sailed into a once-every-20-year storm, with winds in excess of 86 mph and seas with a significant height* of something like 22–26 feet, all but ensuring the *Fitzgerald* was hit by even larger waves, maybe waves higher than 40 feet.[28] (The captain of the *Arthur M. Anderson*, which was tailing the Fitz, reported getting hit by two 35-footers in a row.)[29] Worse yet, the waves were moving west to east, a rare direction for large waves on the lake.

In short, the *Fitzgerald* had the misfortune of sailing directly into the worst part of the storm at the wrong time. All in all, it was the worst possible scenario for a ship that had already lost some freeboard and taken on water.

*Significant wave height refers to the average height of the highest third of the waves present during a given storm.

Shipwrecks and Accidents Today

While the last major shipwreck was the loss of the *Edmund Fitzgerald* in 1975, smaller-scale accidents, sinkings and fatalities have occurred. And while shipping advances have made a large-scale shipwreck less likely, a ship is always one error, mechanical breakdown or an especially bad storm away from potential disaster. For a case in point, consider the *Paul R. Tregurtha*, the largest ship on the Lakes, which ran aground in the St. Marys River in 2014 and blocked traffic for over 24 hours, proving that ship accidents and mishaps are anything but a thing of the past.

Split Rock Lighthouse, lit

A FEW ESPECIALLY BEAUTIFUL SHIPS

Great Lakes freighters are utilitarian vessels, but they are also well-engineered machines and each has a unique style and grace. That's what makes ship watching so endearing; it's not just the sheer scope and size of the vessels that makes ship watching an enjoyable pastime. Ships with clean lines, fresh colors and unique designs, like the *Edward L. Ryerson* (shown at right), offer a reward all their own. Here are a few of my personal favorite vessels on the Lakes. As you ship watch, you'll undoubtedly discover your own fleet of favorites.

The *Edward L. Ryerson*

The *Edward L. Ryerson*

Beloved by many ship watchers, the 730-foot *Ryerson* is arguably the most beautiful ship on the Lakes. Entering service in 1960, she is a straight-decked bulker and features a sleek pilothouse at the front of the ship and a graceful contour. Her sleek red-and-white paint job looks like something out of an Art Deco painting. One of the faster vessels on the Lakes, she is capable of reaching nearly 20 miles per hour, earning her the nickname of the "Fast Eddie."[1] Unfortunately, she has recently been laid up, as her relatively small cargo holds and lack of self-unloading equipment have made operating her uncompetitive in today's market. Her future remains somewhat uncertain.

The *Alpena*

The *Alpena* is the oldest U.S. ship on the Lakes, if you're looking for a ship with a vintage feel, check out the 519-foot *Alpena*. Launched amid World War II in 1942, the *Alpena* was originally an ore carrier and even a saltie for a decade.[2] Today, she's a cement carrier and heads from Superior, Wisconsin, to Hamilton, Ontario.

The *Stewart J. Cort*

The first 1000-footer on the Great Lakes, the *Stewart J. Cort* was launched in 1972. The *Cort* is unique because it is the only modern vessel built in the traditional laker style, with the pilothouse and crew quarters forward and the engine room to the aft. This makes the *Cort* look like something of a throwback; all of the other 1000-footers have their engine room and pilothouse to the rear, and this can make their bows look somewhat stubby, in this author's opinion.

The *St. Marys Challenger*

The *St. Marys Challenger* is no longer in service, but it is worth mentioning because it was one of the more-beloved ships on the lake—and the most durable. Built in 1908, she was in service for over one hundred years on the Great Lakes, being retired in 2013. As disappointing as this is, the ship isn't entirely done yet; her hull is now in use as a barge, so somewhat amazingly she will continue in some form on the Great Lakes.

The *Alpena*

The *St. Marys Challenger*

HISTORY OF LAKE FREIGHTER DESIGN

Shipping technology on the Great Lakes is constantly evolving. Wooden sailing vessels were the primary mode of transportation for centuries, but such vessels were replaced by iron– and then steel–hulled vessels powered by steam, then heavy fuel oil, then diesel. Along the way, the design of the ships themselves changed dramatically. This is a brief look at a few notable examples in the history of Great Lakes freighter design.

S.S. *Meteor*

The lake freighter that we know today is a relatively recent development. The first lake freighter was the *Robert J. Hackett*; she was launched in 1869. Up until that point, cargo had been carried first by sailing vessels, then by steam-powered freighters, but using either type of those vessels proved problematic, as they weren't ideal for the cargoes—iron ore, grain—common on the Great Lakes. In particular, unloading them was inefficient, and as many ships didn't have readily accessible holds, unloading proved difficult. (Such vessels were better suited to transporting lumber, which can be transported on a ship's deck.)

The solution was a new kind of vessel: The bulk freighter. Invented by Captain Eli Peck, the original vessel was something of a hybrid of a sailing vessel and a steamship, but the revolutionary design contained many features found in many Lakers today: the *Hackett's* pilothouse was at the front of the ship and its engine room to the rear. This left ample room for a huge cargo hold; while small when compared to today's 1000-footers, at 210 feet long, she was no small craft.[1] In addition, her hatches were designed to expedite cargo loading and unloading at port.[2]

Nonetheless, the *Hackett* was just the first step in bulk freighter design on the Lakes. She was built with wood, and the introduction of iron, then steel, into shipbuilding really brought ships into the modern era. The *Hackett* was a large ship for her time, but by the turn of the twentieth century, ships more than triple her size were built.

Over time, many classes of vessels were built, but a few especially notable designs dominated much of the history of Great Lakes shipping. One notable design was the whaleback freighter, which resembled something like a whale's back or a submarine above  the surface. Built in the last decades of the nineteenth century, these ships were sturdy, and several dozen were built, remaining in service until the middle of the twentieth century. The lone surviving whaleback freighter is the S.S. *Meteor* (shown on page 163).

Another type of Great Lakes vessel is known as a straight decker. Like the *Hackett* before them, straight deckers have their pilothouse forward and their engine room to the aft, giving them a distinctive profile on the lake. By contrast, 1000-footers usually have the pilothouse and the engine room to the rear of the ship. (The *Stewart J. Cort* is the only exception.)

Straight deckers get their shape in part because of their holds, which head straight down. (Self-unloaders have curving holds that help feed the unloading equipment at the bottom of the hold.) With the rise of self-unloading equipment and the 1000-footers, many straight deckers were scrapped. Today, there are relatively few still in service. Even so, they remain some of the most popular ships on the Lakes.

Ask a Sailor

Doug "Diamondug" LaLonde's career on the Great Lakes spanned over forty years. An avid blogger (www.greatlakesships.net), Mr. LaLonde was kind enough to answer a number of questions about his time on the Great Lakes.

What is your job aboard your present ship? What other positions have you held?

My last position on the *Indiana Harbor* was second mate. In fact, thinking back, I've just realized I've held the second mate's position longer, or more often, than any other.

For quite some time I was first mate. It's a very demanding job and most of the time I wished I wasn't doing it. The first mate has too many responsibilities. He (or she) often loses sleep—staying awake doing payroll or monitoring the loading of the ship.

Most mates are *not* particularly fond of the second mate's job because there's so much paperwork involved. Clerical stuff is right up my alley though, so I always liked it. In fact I still think it's the best job on the ship. Why? It's simple, really: nobody bothers the second mate. If s/he has some experience, the captain usually won't ever interfere. The second mate is kind of like the "invisible" man. Because he works the hours between 12 and 4, the captain and everyone else is usually sleeping during the second mate's midnight watch. So this leaves them on their own, without any interference from anyone! Plus the pay is significantly better than third mate and not much less than the first mate.

What is daily life like on board a ship?

Life on board ship is very different than on the shore. When you get off work, there's nowhere to go! If you're a watchstander, it's even weirder.

A "watchstander" works "watches" in four-hour increments. Either between 4 to 8 (a.m. and p.m.), 8 to 12, or 12 to 4. So, you work for 4 hours and then you're off for 8. That's when life gets weird. Here's why: Almost all watchstanders sleep twice a day. Sleeping only once a day is just about impossible for a watchstander. I think the main reason is that you subconsciously feel that you could be called on to work overtime, sometimes without knowing before-hand. Therefore you sleep between each watch otherwise you just might have to go too long without sleep.

Eventually, you're so accustomed to sleeping twice a day that you don't function very well without your "nap." For many of us this even continues when we're home on vacation.

Which vessels have you served on, and what are a few of your favorites. Why?

I have been on many Great Lakes freighters and there's really no point in mentioning all of them. But I do have *two* favorites. Both are American Steamship Company vessels: The *Sam Laud* and the *Indiana Harbor*. These are the two vessels that I worked on the most during my career.

These ships are literally "legends" in their own time. All boatwatchers (with any experience) have heard of or seen these ships.

The *Sam Laud* is 635 feet long, which is small by today's standards. But it goes to ports that the bigger ships can't get into. The

Cuyahoga River in Cleveland, St. Joseph, Michigan, and way up to the end of the Fox River in Green Bay to name a few.

Life and work on the *Sam Laud* is very fast-paced, and I loved it when I was younger. Sometimes you will load the ship and unload it on the same day. In fact, that often happens.

The *Indiana Harbor* is 1,000 feet long. There are several ports that it can "fit" into but not anywhere near as many as the smaller ships.

Life on the *Indiana Harbor* is much more laid-back and easy. But you do have excitement, now and then.

For the captain, mates and wheelsman, it's *all* about the rivers on a 1000-footer. There are famous turns, especially in the St. Mary's River that have to be done precisely in all kinds of weather conditions.

All Great Lakes pilots are familiar with the Rock Cut, the Moon Island Turn, Johnson's Point, the turn into the Livingston Channel down near Trenton, Michigan, and of course the one I worry about the most: the infamous Amherstburg Channel coming up into the Detroit River System. You *really* have to be on your toes when you're piloting a 1000-foot ship up through the Amherstburg Channel.

But mostly, I liked these two ships because of the crews. The best friends I have on freighters are from the crews on both these vessels.

What do you enjoy doing in your downtime aboard ship?

Even though you're on a ship with 20 or 25 shipmates, you're basically alone. Although you are normally on friendly terms with all the members in the crew, they're not family and they're really not friends, so you're alone.

I have a few hobbies that I do by myself. I like to read and I like being online. I can do both in private in my room. I also like working on a few blogs I run online. And, of course, I practice on my guitar. I've played guitar since I was a young man of about 8 years old.

Then of course, there's food. I eat at least two large meals a day... Lunch and dinner (because of the hours I work), and sometimes I "snack" way too much! The food is usually good and of course it's free.

Last but not least, I call home and communicate online with my friends and family at home. I don't like to admit it, but I miss them a lot while I'm gone.

What's the worst weather you've seen on the Lakes?

It's likely if you work on a ship on the Great Lakes that you will be in rough weather in your first year. You may not be in real bad weather unless you sail for several seasons.

Captains obviously try to avoid heavy seas and wind conditions. Storms can and have sunk ships on the Great Lakes. Any ship can sink if you do dumb things. And a particularly "dumb" thing to do is take any ship out onto any of the Great Lakes when there are storm warnings up.

I personally have been out on the lake/s in extremely rough weather. This usually happened on accident; there were no storm warnings up, or the weather was not predicted to be as bad as it got (which usually is the case).

In dangerously heavy seas you don't usually think that the ship may sink. You're too busy securing the ship and the stuff on the ship. You're too busy trying to do your job and stay on your feet while you're doing it.

The scariest thing about being in heavy seas on a Great Lakes bulk freighter is that the ship "bends" a lot. From the pilothouse (or from other places on the ship), you can see the bending very well. Yes, steel ships bend, and obviously, if they bend too much they can break.

The U.S. Coast Guard determined that the *Edmund Fitzgerald* did not "break up" before it went down. All Great Lakes Seamen (with experience) believe that it broke at the surface of the water and that is what caused it to go down.

I don't know if I've ever been on a ship that "nearly sank" in rough weather. But, I have been on ships in rough weather when I wished that I wasn't there.

Even with the "new" exposure suits that will keep you warm and floating should you end up in the water during a winter storm (if you can get it on in time), I still don't believe that many would survive a sinking on the Great Lakes such as the *Fitzgerald* experienced.

How has the shipping industry—and that of the U.S. fleet, especially—changed during your career?

I first started "shipping out" in 1972; I was 18 years old. My first ship was the S.S. *Harris N. Snyder.* It was a steamship and it was in pretty bad shape. It was owned by the Boland & Cornelius Steamship Company, which later became the American Steamship Company.

The S.S. *Harris N. Snyder* was a small ship by today's standards. It was in the neighborhood of 600 feet long and probably 67 feet wide. We carried limestone and gypsum, coal and on occasion, taconite.

I was a deckhand, back when they were still called deckhands. Today, the Ordinary Seamen are called GUDEs (general utility deck or engine department) on American Steamship Company vessels. And there are a lot fewer of them on a ship now than there were in 1972. In fact, there are a lot fewer seamen in all capacities on a modern Great Lakes bulk freighter.

What has changed for the better in your career? What has changed for the worse?

The Great Lakes bulk freighters nowadays are larger and easier to live and work on. I think, however, that there is a lot more personal, emotional stress on a freighter these days.

There is a lot more government control and the policies of the companies have obviously changed considerably through the years. Now a seaman must have more documentation to work on a ship, whether on the Great Lakes or anywhere else. To work on a ship, you should have a U.S. Passport, and you need a TWIC (Transportation Workers Identity Card). Of course you also need Merchant Mariner documents, and while they were once good indefinitely, they now must be renewed every five years. If you are an officer, the paperwork and documentation is considerably more complicated.

There are three entities involved in all Merchant Marine employ-ment these days. They are: the government, the company and the union. The amount of paperwork and policies between all these organizations can literally drive you crazy.

But to be honest—I still *love* Sailing—and I miss it a little, since I've retired.

Glossary

AIS: Automatic Identification System. A "transponder" of sorts that tracks each individual vessel on the Great Lakes, transmitting its position, speed and other details every few minutes. AIS-tracking websites like www.marinetraffic.com and ais.boatnerd.com are invaluable tools for ship watchers, as they let one know where a ship is and help predict when to expect it.

Bow thruster: An inset propeller on the front or back of a ship that helps a large vessel maneuver more effectively.

Checked down: A ship that has slowed down in speed.

Downbound: A ship that is headed "down" the Lakes toward the Atlantic Ocean. For example, a ship heading from Lake Superior to Lake Huron is considered downbound.

Draught markings: A series of hash marks on the side of a ship that allows observers to know how low the ship is riding in the water.

Gearless: A Great Lakes ship lacking self-unloading equipment; such ships are usually called "straight deckers."

Laker: A U.S.- or Canadian-owned lake freighter that operates on the Great Lakes.

Pilot: A specialized sailor who guides a ship through areas that are difficult to navigate or congested. A pilot is an expert in the area where they sail. All saltwater vessels require pilots on the Great Lakes.

Plimsoll line: Found toward the middle of the ship, the Plimsoll line is a marking consisting of a number of lines, each of which corresponds to water's density under certain conditions (tropical, freshwater, winter in the North Atlantic, etc.). Water density is a very important characteristic when determining how much cargo can be loaded onto a ship, as it affects how low a ship rides in the water.

Port of registry: The country where a ship is registered. Registration fees and taxes vary by country, and some companies choose to register their ships in other countries in order to pay the lower fees. U.S. companies are prohibited from doing so because of the Jones Act, a law that requires U.S. ships to be owned by U.S. companies.

Saltie: A saltwater vessel visiting the Great Lakes.

Self-unloader: A ship that carries equipment (conveyor belts, a boom) to unload its cargo without the help of gear onshore.

Stack markings: The combination of letters and geographic symbols found on a given ship's smokestack. Each company has its own unique stack marking.

Straight decker: A Great Lakes freighter that lacks unloading equipment; they usually have a pilothouse at the front and the engine at the rear.

Taconite: A low-grade iron ore that is turned into "taconite pellets," small marble-sized pieces of material that consist of about 65 percent iron. When ships are carrying iron ore, they are usually carrying taconite.

Tall ship: A traditionally rigged sailing vessel; the Great Lakes are occasionally visited by tall ships.

Thousand-footer: A Great Lakes vessel that is 1,000 feet or longer; all 1000-footers are owned by U.S. companies.

Upbound: A ship headed "up" the Lakes toward the west. For example, a ship heading from Lake Huron to Lake Superior is considered "upbound."

Whaleback: A type of freighter popular in the 1910s and 1920s, whalebacks looked something like a cross between a submarine and a surfaced whale.

For More Information

Government Organizations/General Information

National Oceanographic and Atmospheric Administration (www.noaa.gov)

Great Lakes Information Network (www.great-lakes.net)

U.S. Coast Guard, Ninth District (www.uscg.mil/d9/)

U.S. Department of Transportation, Maritime Administration (www.marad.dot.gov)

U.S. Army Corps of Engineers, Detroit District (www.lre.usace.army.mil)

Great Lakes Seaway Corporation (www.greatlakes-seaway.com)

St. Lawrence Seaway Development Corporation (www.seaway.dot.gov)

The St. Lawrence Seaway Management Company (www.seaway.ca/)

Welland Canal Information (www.wellandcanal.com)

Ship Tracking Websites and Current Conditions

Boatnerd AIS (ais.boatnerd.com)

Marine Traffic (www.marinetraffic.com)

National Data Buoy Center (www.ndbc.noaa.gov)

Great Lakes Environmental Research Laboratory, Great Lakes Ice Cover (www.glerl.noaa.gov/data/ice/)

Great Lakes Museums

Dossin Great Lakes Museum (http://detroithistorical.org)

Great Lakes Shipwreck Museum (www.shipwreckmuseum.com)

Great Lakes Historical Society (www.inlandseas.org)

Great Lakes Naval Museum
(www.history.navy.mil/museums/greatlakes/index.htm)

Great Lakes Science Center (www.greatscience.com)

Museum Ships

Edna G. tugboat (http://lakecountyhistoricalsociety.org/museums/
view/edna-g.-tugboat)

William G. Mather freighter (www.greatscience.com/exhibits/
steamship-william-g-mather.aspx)

S.S. *William A. Irvin* freighter (www.decc.org/william-a-irvin/)

S.S. *Meteor* whaleback freighter
(http://superiorpublicmuseums.org/s-s-meteor-2/)

Huron Lightship (www.phmuseum.org/huron-lightship)

U.S. Coast Guard icebreaker *Mackinaw* (www.themackinaw.org)

Accidents/Shipwrecks

David Swayze's Great Lakes Shipwreck File
(www.ship-wreck.com/shipwreck/swayze/)

U.S. Coast Guard Incident Investigation Reports
(https://cgmix.uscg.mil/iir/)

U.S. Coast Guard Marine Casualty Reports
(https://homeport.uscg.mil/marinecasualtyreports)

Michigan Underwater Preserves (www.michiganpreserves.org)

Tall Ships

Tall Ships Challenge (www.sailtraining.org)

Sail Training Vessel Database; search by state to find vessels
near you (www.sailtraining.org/membervessels/database.php)

Books

Hale, Dennis. *Sole Survivor: Dennis Hale's Own Story*. Lakeshore Charters & Marine Explorations, Inc. 2002.

Ratigan, William. *Great Lakes Shipwrecks & Survivals*. William B. Eerdmans Publishing. 1977.

Riedel, Franz A. *Commercial Ships on the Great Lakes: A Photo Gallery*. Hudson: Enthusiast Books. 2005.

Thompson, Mark L. *Graveyard of the Great Lakes*. Detroit: Wayne State University Press. 2004.

More Detailed Information

Boatnerd (www.boatnerd.com)

Know Your Ships (http://knowyourships.com)

Great Lakes Tugs and Workboats (https://gltugs.wordpress.com)

Tugboat Enthusiasts' Society (www.tugboatenthusiastsociety.org)

The Great Lakes Ship Site (www.greatlakesships.net)

Selected Shipping Companies and Organizations
U.S.

Lake Carriers' Association (www.lcaships.com)

American Steamship Company (www.americansteamship.com)

The Interlake Steamship Company (www.inter-lakesteamship.com)

Great Lakes Fleet, operated as a subsidiary of Canadian National out of Duluth (http://cn.ca)

Canadian

Canadian Shipowners Association (http://shipowners.ca)

Algoma Central Corporation (www.algonet.com)

Canadian Steamship Lines (http://www.cslships.com)

Works Cited

Map/Ports on the Lake

1. U.S. Department of Transportation, Maritime Transportation. "Status of the U.S.–Flag Great Lakes Water Transportation Industry, 2013. Final Report." Washington D.C.: U.S. Department of Transportation. www.marad.dot.gov/documents/US-Flag_Great_Lakes_Water_Transportation_Industry_Final_Report_2013.pdf

2. Great Lakes St. Lawrence Seaway System. "Seaway Map." Washington D.C.: U.S. Department of Transportation. 2015. http://www.great-lakes-seaway.com/en/navigating/map/index.html

Starting Out Ship Watching

1. Boatnerd.com. "Foreign Ship Data & Photo Gallery: 2014 Season." Port Huron: Boatnerd. www.boatnerd.com/pictures/salty/

2. Great Lakes Information Network, Great Lakes Commission. Great Lakes Ports and Shipping. "Flags." Ann Arbor: Great Lakes Commission. www.great-lakes.net/teach/business/ship/ship_2.html

3. Great Lakes Information Network. Great Lakes Ports and Shipping. "Fleets and stack insignia." Ann Arbor: Great Lakes Commission. www.great-lakes.net/teach/business/ship/ship_2.html

4. Boatnerd.com "Great Lakes & Seaway Shipping Online Vessel Passage Maps" Port Huron: Boatnerd. 2015. ais.boatnerd.com

5. Marinetraffic.com. "Live Ships Map– AIS –Vessel Traffic and Positions – AIS Marine Traffic." 2015. www.marinetraffic.com/en/

Ship Watching FAQs

1. U.S. Department of Transportation, Maritime Transportation. "Status of the U.S.–Flag Great Lakes Water Transportation Industry, 2013. Final Report." Washington D.C.: U.S. Department of Transportation. www.marad.dot.gov/documents/US-Flag_Great_Lakes_Water_Transportation_Industry_Final_Report_2013.pdf

The Basics

1. Great Lakes St. Lawrence Seaway System. "Seaway Map." Washington D.C.: Saint Lawrence Seaway Development Corporation (U.S.A.) 2014. www.greatlakes-seaway.com/en/navigating/map/index.html

2. *Ibid.*

3. Maritime-connector. "Seawaymax." Rijeka (Croatia): Maritime-connector. 2014. http://maritime-connector.com/wiki/seawaymax/

4. Great Lakes St. Lawrence Seaway System. "Seaway Map." Washington D.C.: Saint Lawrence Seaway Development Corporation (U.S.A.) 2014. www.greatlakes-seaway.com/en/navigating/map/index.html

5. Boatnerd.com. *Paul R. Tregurtha* "Queen of the Lakes." Port Huron: Boatnerd. 2015. www.boatnerd.com/pictures/fleet/prtrgrth.htm

6. Chamber of Marine Commerce. "Great Lakes Ships & Carriers." Ottawa: Chamber of Marine Commerce. www.marinedelivers.com/great-lakes-ships-carriers

7. Boatnerd.com "Great Lakes & Seaway Shipping Online Vessel Passage Maps." Port Huron: Boatnerd. 2015. Ais.boatnerd.com.

8. Boatnerd.com. "Great Lakes Fleet Photo Gallery." Port Huron: Boatnerd. 2014. www.boatnerd.com/pictures/fleet/

9. U.S. Department of Transportation, Maritime Transportation. "Status of the U.S.-Flag Great Lakes Water Transportation Industry, 2013. Final Report." Washington D.C.: U.S. Department of Transportation. www.marad.dot.gov/documents/US-Flag_Great_Lakes_Water_Transportation_Industry_Final_Report_2013.pdf

Types of Ships

1. American Steamship Company. "Self-unloading technology." Williamsville: American Steamship Company. 2014. www.americansteamship.com/self-unloading-technology.php

2. Maritime-connector. "Bulk carrier (sizes)." Rijeka (Croatia): Maritime-connector. 2014. http://maritime-connector.com/bulk-carrier/

3. Algoma Central Corporation. "Gearless Bulk Carriers. St. Catharines: Algoma Central Corporation." 2015. www.algonet.com/Business-Units/Domestic-Shipping/Gearless-Bulk-Carriers/

4. Lipinski, Patrick. "From one-time oddball to the latest new thing on the Lakes." North Star Port. Spring 2012. www.inlandmariners.com/Mariners_06/im_library_articles_files/Tug/barges.pdf

5. *Ibid*.

6. Pennock, Isaac. Great Lakes Tugs & Workboats. "*Edward H*. Tugboat." 2015. https://gltugs.wordpress.com/edward-h/

7. Pennock, Isaac. Great Lakes Tugs & Workboats. "U.S. Army Corps of Engineers." 2015. https://gltugs.wordpress.com/u-s-army-corps-of-engineers/

8. Pennock, Isaac. Great Lakes Tugs & Workboats. "*Jill Marie*." 2015. https://gltugs.wordpress.com/jill-marie/

9. Martino, Tommy. "HHL *Elbe* the latest cargo ship carrying wind turbine parts to arrive in Muskegon." July 8, 2014. Grand Rapids: *Michigan Live*. www.mlive.com/news/muskegon/index.ssf/2014/07/hhl_elbe_the_latest_cargo_ship.html

10. U.S. Coast Guard. "Aircraft, Boats, and Cutters: Cutters, 240-foot Seagoing Buoy Tender/ Icebreaker (WLBB-30)" Washington, D.C.: U.S. Coast Guard. 2015. www.uscg.mil/datasheet/240mack.asp

11. U.S. Coast Guard. "USCGC *BUCKTHORN* (WLI 642)" Washington, D.C.: U.S. Coast Guard. 2015. www.uscg.mil/d9/sectsaultstemarie/cgcbuckthorn.asp

12. Visit Duluth. "Tall Ships." Duluth: Visit Duluth. www.visitduluth.com/tallships/

The U.S. & Canadian Fleets

1. Lake Carriers' Association. 2012 Statistical Annual Report of Lake Carriers' Association. " Vessel Rosters." www.lcaships.com/wp-content/uploads/2013/03/VESSEL-ROSTERS-PART-II.pdf

2. *Ibid.*

3. *Ibid.*

4. Boatnerd.com. "Great Lakes Fleet Photo Gallery." Port Huron: Boatnerd. 2014. www.boatnerd.com/pictures/fleet/

5. CSL Group. "CSL'S Trillium Class Laker." 2015. www.cslships.com/en/media-center/brochures/csls-trillium-class-laker-0

6. Boatnerd.com. "Great Lakes Fleet Photo Gallery." Port Huron: Boatnerd. 2014. www.boatnerd.com/pictures/fleet/

7. *Ibid.*

U.S. Ports & Cargo

1. U.S. Department of Transportation, Maritime Transportation. "Status of the U.S.-Flag Great Lakes Water Transportation Industry, 2013. Final Report." Washington D.C.: U.S. Department of Transportation. www.marad.dot.gov/documents/US-Flag_Great_Lakes_Water_Transportation_Industry_Final_Report_2013.pdf

2. *Ibid.*

3. Lake Carriers' Association. "2013 Annual Report of the Lake Carriers' Association: U.S.-Flag Shipments of Dry-Bulk Cargoes on the Great Lakes Calendar Years 2008-2013 and 5-Year Average." www.lcaships.com/wp-content/uploads/2014/07/60005_60005-LCA_p1-4.pdf

4. U.S. Department of Transportation, Maritime Transportation. "Status of the U.S.-Flag Great Lakes Water Transportation Industry, 2013. Final Report." Washington D.C.: U.S. Department of Transportation. www.marad.dot.gov/documents/US-Flag_Great_Lakes_Water_Transportation_Industry_Final_Report_2013.pdf

5. Great Northern Iron Ore Properties. "The Mining Process as it pertains to the Trust of Great Northern Iron Ore Properties." 2015. www.gniop.com/mining.html

6. U.S. Department of the Interior, U.S. Geological Survey. "The National Coal Resource Assessment Review, Chapter H." Reston: U.S. Geological Survey. 2009. http://pubs.usgs.gov/pp/1625f/downloads/ChapterH.pdf

7. U.S. Department of Transportation, Maritime Transportation. "Status of the U.S.–Flag Great Lakes Water Transportation Industry, 2013. Final Report." Washington D.C.: U.S. Department of Transportation. www.marad.dot.gov/documents/US-Flag_Great_Lakes_Water_Transportation_Industry_Final_Report_2013.pdf

8. Northland News Center. "Great Lakes Coal Shipments Down." October 24, 2013. www.northlandsnewscenter.com/news/local/Coal-shipments-from-the-Great-Lakes-are-down-13-from-last-year--228998601.html

9. U.S. Department of Transportation, Maritime Transportation. "Status of the U.S.–Flag Great Lakes Water Transportation Industry, 2013. Final Report." Washington D.C.: U.S. Department of Transportation. www.marad.dot.gov/documents/US-Flag_Great_Lakes_Water_Transportation_Industry_Final_Report_2013.pdf

10. *Ibid.*

11. *Ibid.*

12. Lake Carriers' Association. "An Overview of Our Industry: Great Lakes Shipping." 2015. www.lcaships.com/industry/

13. National Association of Wheat Growers. "Wheat Info: Fast Facts." 2013. www.wheatworld.org/wheat-info/fast-facts/

14. Duluth Seaway Port Authority. "The largest, farthest-inland freshwater port." 2015. www.duluthport.com/port.php

15. Illinois International Port District. "Facts and Statistics." 2015. www.iipd.com/about/facts-stats.htm

16. Ports of Indiana. "Ports of Indiana/About Us/FAQs." 2013. www.portsofindiana.com/poi/about_us/faqs.cfm

17. U.S. Department of Transportation, Maritime Transportation. "Status of the U.S.–Flag Great Lakes Water Transportation Industry, 2013. Final Report." Washington D.C.: U.S. Department of Transportation. www.marad.dot.gov/documents/US-Flag_Great_Lakes_Water_Transportation_Industry_Final_Report_2013.pdf

18. U.S. Army Corps of Engineers, Navigation and Civil Works Decision Support Center. "The U.S. Waterway System, Transportation Facts and Information." November 2013. www.navigationdatacenter.us/factcard/factcard13.pdf

19. Port of Cleveland. "Maritime & Logistics Overview." 2015. www.portofcleveland.com/maritime-logistics/

Foreign Ships

1. Great Lakes Information Network, Great Lakes Commission. Great Lakes Ports and Shipping. "Flags." Ann Arbor: Great Lakes Commission. www.great-lakes.net/teach/business/ship/ship_2.html

2. *Ibid.*

3. Boatnerd.com. "Foreign Ship Data & Photo Gallery: 2014 Season." Port Huron: Boatnerd. www.boatnerd.com/pictures/salty/

4. *Ibid.*

Understanding Ship Whistles

1. U.S. Coast Guard, Navigation Center: The Navigation Center for Excellence. " Rule 34: Maneuvering and Warning Signals." Alexandria: Department of Homeland Security, U.S. Coast Guard. 2015. www.navcen.uscg.gov/?pageName=Rule34

2. *Ibid.*

3. *Ibid.*

4. U.S. Coast Guard, Navigation Center: The Navigation Center for Excellence. "Rule 35: Maneuvering and Warning Signals." Alexandria: Department of Homeland Security, U.S. Coast Guard. 2015. www.navcen.uscg.gov/?pageName=Rule35

5. U.S. Coast Guard, Navigation Center: The Navigation Center for Excellence. " Rule 34: Maneuvering and Warning Signals." Alexandria: Department of Homeland Security, U.S. Coast Guard. 2015. www.navcen.uscg.gov/?pageName=Rule34

6. Great Lakes Information Network, Great Lakes Commission. Great Lakes Ports and Shipping. "Whistle blasts...what do they mean?" Ann Arbor: Great Lakes Commission. www.great-lakes.net/teach/business/ship/ship_2.html

Ship Markings

1. National Oceanographic and Atmospheric Administration, National Ocean Service. "What is a Plimsoll line?" 2015. http://oceanservice.noaa.gov/facts/plimsoll-line.html

2. Bray, Patrick. "The Bulbous Bow." Diesel Duck: Martin's Marine Engineering Page. 2008. www.dieselduck.info/library/01%20articles/bulbous_bows.htm

Stack Markings and Color Schemes

1. Great Lakes Information Network, Great Lakes Commission. Great Lakes Ports and Shipping. "Fleets and stack insignia." Ann Arbor: Great Lakes Commission. www.great-lakes.net/teach/business/ship/ship_2.html

2. Canadian National. "CN Great Lakes Fleet." 2015. http://cn.ca/greatlakesfleet

3. The Interlake Steamship Company. "Our Fleet." 2015. www.interlake-steamship.com/index.php/our-fleet.html

4. American Steamship Company. "American Steamship Company Vessels." 2015. www.americansteamship.com/fleet/index.php

Navigation

1. United States Coast Guard, Office of Boating Safety. "U.S. Aids to Navigation System." www.uscg.mil/d13/dpw/docs/usaidstonavigationsystembooklet23dec03.pdf

2. *Ibid*.

3. National Oceanographic and Atmospheric Administration. Coast Pilot 6: Great Lakes: Lakes Ontario, Erie, Huron, Michigan, and Superior and St. Lawrence River. (41st edition.) 2011. www.nauticalcharts.noaa.gov/nsd/coastpilot/archive/6/CP6-41ed-2011-reduced.pdf

4. United States Coast Guard. "Nationwide Automatic Identification System." 2014. www.uscg.mil/acquisition/nais/

5. National Oceanographic and Atmospheric Administration. Coast Pilot 6: Great Lakes: Lakes Ontario, Erie, Huron, Michigan, and Superior and St. Lawrence River. (41st edition.) 2011. www.nauticalcharts.noaa.gov/nsd/coastpilot/archive/6/CP6-41ed-2011-reduced.pdf

6. Boatnerd.com. "Estimated Freighter Travel Times – Major Ports." Port Huron: Boatnerd. http://boatnerd.com/facts-figures/travel_times-lakes.htm

7. National Oceanographic and Atmospheric Administration. Great Lakes Environmental Research Laboratory. "Great Lakes Ice Cover." 2014. www.glerl.noaa.gov/data/ice/

8. Kirchner, Paul G. "Careers in the Merchant Marine: A Career as a Ship Pilot." *Proceedings of the Marine Safety and Security Council*. Fall 2008. Washington D.C.: U.S. Coast Guard. www.uscg.mil/proceedings/fall2008/articles/9%20SHIP%20PILOT.PDF

Life Aboard Ship

1. Great Lakes Information Network, Great Lakes Commission. Great Lakes Ports and Shipping. "Vessel Types." Ann Arbor: Great Lakes Commission. www.great-lakes.net/teach/business/ship/ship_2.html

2. LaLonde, Doug. The Great Lakes Ship Site. "What is a Great Lakes Pilot? www.greatlakesships.net/what-is-a-great-lakes-pilot/

3. *Ibid*.

4. *Ibid*.

5. United States Maritime Center, U.S. Coast Guard. "Credential Application Process." www.uscg.mil/nmc/credentials/default.asp

6. Boatnerd.com. "Great Lakes Fleet Page Vessel Feature -- Paul R. Tregurtha." Port Huron: Boatnerd. 2015. www.boatnerd.com/pictures/fleet/prtrgrth.htm

7. Lake Carriers' Association. "Shipboard Employment Opportunities." 2015. www.lcaships.com/careers/

8. Bureau of Labor Statistics. "Census of Fatal Occupational Injuries (CFOI) – Current and Revised Data." September 11, 2014. www.bls.gov/iif/oshcfoi1.htm

Where to Watch, Lake Superior
Duluth

1. Go Duluth MN. "Duluth Aerial Lift Bridge." 2012. www.goduluthmn.com/aerial-lift-bridge.html

2. Cowardin, David. Duluthoutdoors.com "Minnesota Point (Park Point)." 2015. http://duluthoutdoors.com/minnesota-point-park-point/

3. Superior, Wisconsin (Official Website). "Wisconsin Point." 2015. www.ci.superior.wi.us/index.aspx?NID=226

4. City of Duluth. "Skyline Parkway Scenic Byway." 2015. www.skylineparkway.org

5. Minnesota Historical Society, Historic Sites. "Split Rock Lighthouse." 2015. http://sites.mnhs.org/historic-sites/split-rock-lighthouse

6. Duluth Entertainment Convention Center. "SS *William A. Irvin*." 2010. www.decc.org/william-a-irvin/

7. Superior Public Museums. "SS *Meteor*." 2015. http://superiorpublicmuseums.org/s-s-meteor-2/

The Soo Locks, Sault Ste. Marie, MI

1. Sault Ste. Marie, Michigan. "Soo Locks Visitor Center." 2015. www.saultstemarie.com/member-3/soo-locks-visitor-center-1.html

2. Sault Ste. Marie, Michigan. "Soo Locks Boat Tours." 2015. www.saultstemarie.com/soo-locks-boat-tours-52/

3. Trip Advisor. "Clyde's Drive-In." 2015. www.tripadvisor.com/Restaurant_Review-g42684-d1535075-Reviews-Clyde_s_Drive_In-Sault_Ste_Marie_Michigan.html

4. Share the Sault: What To Do in the "Soo." "Dunbar Park." August 2008. http://sharethesault.blogspot.com/2008/08/dunbar-park.html

5. Great Lakes Shipwreck Museum. "*Edmund Fitzgerald*." 2015. www.shipwreckmuseum.com/edmundfitzgerald

Where to Watch, Lake Michigan
St. Ignace and Mackinaw City, MI

1. Mackinac Bridge Authority. "About the Bridge." 2015. www.mackinacbridge.org/about-the-bridge-8/

2. Boatnerd.com "Vessel Passage." Port Huron: Boatnerd. 2015. www.boatnerd.com/passage/defaultpassage.htm 3. Mackinac Island Tourism Bureau. "Mackinaw Island." 2015. http://www.mackinacisland.org/activities/parks-historic-sites-museums/

3. Mackinac Bridge Authority. "About the Bridge." 2015. www.mackinacbridge.org/about-the-bridge-8/

4. Mackinac State Historic Parks. "Old Mackinac Point Lighthouse." 2015. www.mackinacparks.com/parks-and-attractions/old-mackinac-point-lighthouse/

6. Michigan Underwater Preserve Council. Straits of Mackinac Shipwreck Preserve. "Cedarville/Sandusky." 2010. www.michiganpreserves.org/straits.htm

7. *Ibid*.

8. Mackinac State Historic Parks. "Fort Mackinac." 2015. www.mackinacparks.com/parks-and-attractions/fort-mackinac/

9. U.S. Coast Guard. "USCGC *MACKINAW* History. A Brief History on *MACKINAW* (WAGB-83) and *MACKINAW* (WLBB-30)." 2014. www.uscg.mil/d9/cgcMackinaw/history.asp

The South Shore of Lake Michigan

1. Google Earth. "Chicago, 41 43'39.04 N. 87 23'28.92 W." January 14, 2015.

2. Ship Watcher "Gyroplanes" (personal correspondence). October, 2014. Gyroplanes

3. Ports of Indiana Burns Harbor. "Harbor Map." www.portsofindiana.com/BurnsHarborPortFlyer.pdf

4. 2015 Indiana Dunes Tourism. "Official Indiana Dunes Travel Guide." 2015. www.indianadunes.com

5. Chicago Christmas Ship. "*Rouse Simmons*." 2014. http://christmasship.org/index.php?option=com_content&view=article&id=84&Itemid=27

6. *Ibid.*

Where to Watch, Lake Huron
DeTour Passage

1. Michigan Department of Natural Resources. "DeTour State Dock." 2015. www.michigan.gov/dnr/0,4570,7-153-10365_10884_18317-44283--,00.html

2. Historical Society of Museum. "DeTour Passage Historical Museum." www.hsmichigan.org/resources/local-historical-organizations/detour-passage-historical-museum/

3. Drummond Island Tourism Association. "Catching the Drummond Island Ferry." 2015. www.drummondislandchamber.com/index.php?page=Transportation

4. DeTour Reef Light Preservation Society. "Main Page." 2015. http://drlps.com

5. Michigan Underwater Preserve Council. "DeTour Passage Underwater Preserve." 2010. www.michiganpreserves.org/detour.htm

6. *Ibid.*

Where to Watch, Port Huron

1. Acheson Ventures. "Visit the Maritime Center at Vantage Point." 2015. www.achesonventures.com/MaritimeCenter.aspx

2. Boatnerd.com. "Foreign Ship Data & Photo Gallery: 2014 Season." Port Huron: Boatnerd. www.boatnerd.com/pictures/salty/

3. Acheson Ventures. "Visit the Maritime Center at Vantage Point." 2015. www.achesonventures.com/MaritimeCenter.aspx

4. The Blueways of St. Clair. "Thomas Edison Parkway." 2015. www.bluewaysofstclair.org/recreation.asp?ait=av&aid=932

5. Port Huron Museum. "Fort Gratiot Lighthouse." 2015. www.phmuseum.org/fort-gratiot-lighthouse/

6. *Ibid.*

7. Port Huron Museum. "*Huron* Lightship." 2015. www.phmuseum.org/huron-lightship/

Where to Watch, Lake Erie
Detroit

1. www.michigan.gov/dnr/0,4570,7-153-10365_67024---,00.html

2. Bailey, Kenneth (personal communication). October 2014.

3. Anonymous Wyandotte resident (personal communication). October 2014.

4. The Henry Ford. "Ford Rouge Factory Tour." 2015. www.thehenryford.org/rouge/index.aspx

5. *Ibid.*

6. The Henry Ford. "Greenfield Village." 2015. www.thehenryford.org/village/index.aspx

7. Detroit Historical Society. "Dossin Great Lakes Museum, Plan Your Visit." 2015. http://detroithistorical.org/dossin-great-lakes-museum/plan-your-visit/general-information

Cleveland, OH

1. Wendy Park. "Ohio's new Wendy Park...on the shores of Lake Erie in downtown Cleveland." 2015. http://wendypark.org

2. Whiskey Island Marina. "Whiskey Island Marina." 2015. www.whiskey-islandmarina.com

3. *Ibid.*

4. Great Lakes Science Center. "Steamship *William. G. Mather.*" 2015. www.greatscience.com/exhibits/steamship-william-g-mather.aspx

5. National Parks Service. "Cuyahoga Valley National Park: Along the Crooked River." 2015. www.nps.gov/cuva/index.htm

6. *Ibid.*

Where to Watch, Lake Ontario
Northern New York: Eisenhower Lock Visitor Center

1. St. Lawrence Seaway Development Corporation. "St. Lawrence Seaway Eisenhower Lock Visitors' Center Informational Video." 2014. www.seaway.dot.gov/video/st-lawrence-seaway-eisenhower-lock-visitors-center-informational-video

Canada: St. Catharines, Welland, Port Colborne and the Welland Canal

1. Raso, Anthony. "Brief History." www.wellandcanal.com/hist.htm

2. *Ibid.*

3. *Ibid.*

4. City of St. Catharines, the Garden City. "St. Catharines Museum and Welland Canals Centre." 2015. www.stcatharines.ca/en/St-Catharines-Museum.asp

5. Niagara Green Belt. "Lock 7 Viewing Complex." 2015. www.niagaragreenbelt.com/listings/17-canals/308-lock-7-viewing-complex-.html

The U.S. Laker Fleet

1. Lake Carriers' Association. 2012 Statistical Annual Report of Lake Carrier's Association. "Vessel Rosters." www.lcaships.com/wp-content/uploads/2013/03/VESSEL-ROSTERS-PART-II.pdf

2. *Ibid.*

3. *Ibid.*

4. *Ibid.*

5. *Ibid.*

6. U.S. Department of Transportation, Maritime Transportation. "Status of the U.S.-Flag Great Lakes Water Transportation Industry, 2013. Final Report." Washington D.C.: U.S. Department of Transportation. www.marad.dot.gov/documents/US-Flag_Great_Lakes_Water_Transportation_Industry_Final_Report_2013.pdf

7. VanEnkevort Tug and Barge, Inc. "VanEnkevort Tug & Barge, Inc." www.vtbarge.com

About 1000-Footers

1. Lake Carriers' Association. 2012 Statistical Annual Report of Lake Carriers' Association. "Vessel Rosters." www.lcaships.com/wp-content/uploads/2013/03/VESSEL-ROSTERS-PART-II.pdf

2. *Ibid.*

3. *Ibid.*

4. Interlake Steamship Company. "Interlake Steamship's History." 2015. www.interlake-steamship.com/index.php/about-us/history.html

5. Lake Carriers' Association. 2012 Statistical Annual Report of Lake Carrier's Association. "Vessel Rosters." www.lcaships.com/wp-content/uploads/2013/03/VESSEL-ROSTERS-PART-II.pdf

6. U.S. Army Corps of Engineers. "Great Lakes Navigation System: Economic Strength of the Nation." Detroit: U.S. Army Corps, Detroit District. March 2013. www.lre.usace.army.mil/Portals/69/docs/Navigation/GLN_Strength%20to%20the%20Nation%20Booklet2013v2_final2w.pdf

7. *Ibid.*

8. *Ibid.*

Paul R. Tregurtha

1. Boatnerd.com. "*Paul R. Tregurtha* "Queen of the Lakes." Port Huron: Boatnerd. 2015. www.boatnerd.com/pictures/fleet/prtrgrth.htm

2. *Ibid.*

3. The Interlake Steamship Company. "*M/V Paul R. Tregurtha*." 2015. www.interlake-steamship.com/index.php/our-fleet/mv-paul-r-tregurtha.html

4. *Ibid.*

5. Lake Carriers' Association. 2012 Statistical Annual Report of Lake Carriers' Association. "Vessel Rosters." www.lcaships.com/wp-content/uploads/2013/03/VESSEL-ROSTERS-PART-II.pdf

6. The Interlake Steamship Company. "*M/V Paul R. Tregurtha*." 2015. www.interlake-steamship.com/index.php/our-fleet/mv-paul-r-tregurtha.html

7. Boatnerd.com. "*Paul R. Tregurtha* Queen of the Lakes." Port Huron: Boatnerd. 2015. www.boatnerd.com/pictures/fleet/prtrgrth.htm

8. *Ibid.*

9. *Ibid*

10. Rose, Lynn. U.S. Army Corps of Engineers (press release). "Corps to clear channel where ship went aground." August 6, 2012. www.lre.usace.army.mil/Media/NewsReleases/tabid/11351/Article/8167/corps-to-clear-channel-where-ship-went-aground.aspx

11. *Ibid.*

12. U.S. Coast Guard, Ninth District (press release). "Salvage Experts Refloat Grounded Freighter in St. Marys River August 16, 2012." www.uscgnews.com/go/doc/4007/1517635/

13. *Ibid.*

The Indiana Harbor

1. ArcelorMittal. "ArcelorMittal Indiana Harbor." 2015. http://usa.arcelormittal.com/Our-operations/Flat/Indiana-Harbor/

2. Lake Carriers' Association. 2012 Statistical Annual Report of Lake Carrier's Association. "2012 Cargo Records." www.lcaships.com/wp-content/uploads/2013/03/cargo-records.pdf

3. American Steamship Company. "*M/V Indiana Harbor*." 2015. www.americansteamship.com/fleet/mv-indiana-harbor.php

4. *Ibid*.

5. Boatnerd.com. "Great Lakes Fleet Page Vessel Feature – Indiana Harbor." Port Huron: Boatnerd. 2015. www.boatnerd.com/pictures/fleet/prtrgrth.htm

6. *Ibid*.

7. American Steamship Company. "*M/V Indiana Harbor*." 2015. www.americansteamship.com/fleet/mv-indiana-harbor.php

8. *Ibid*.

9. *Ibid*.

10. *Ibid*.

11. *Ibid*.

12. National Oceanographic and Atmospheric Administration, Office of Coast Survey. "Chart 14911." Washington D.C.: National Oceanographic and Atmospheric Administration. 2015. www.charts.noaa.gov/OnLineViewer/14911.shtml

13. U.S. Coast Guard. "Investigation Activity Report: *INDIANA HARBOR*; Grounding. MISLE Activity Number: 119946." July 24, 2009. http://cgmix.uscg.mil/iir/IIRSearchResults.aspx

The *Presque Isle*

1. *Duluth Shipping News*. "Presque Isle." 2015. http://duluthshippingnews.com/ship0322/

2. *Ibid*.

3. Canadian National (brochure). "Great Lakes Fleet." http://cn.ca/-/media/Files/Our%20Business/supply-chain-services/Great-Lakes-Fleet-Brochure-EN.pdf

4. *Ibid*.

5. *Ibid*.

6. *Ibid*.

7. National Oceanographic and Atmospheric Administration. Great Lakes Environmental Research Laboratory. "Great Lakes Ice Cover." 2014. www.glerl.noaa.gov/data/ice/

8. KBJR News. "Shipping season pushes forward despite shifting wind, historic ice." March 31, 2014. www.northlandsnewscenter.com/news/local/Shipping-season-pushes-forward-despite-shifting-wind-historic-ice-253299951.html

Arthur M. Anderson

1. Lake Carriers' Association. 2012 Statistical Annual Report of Lake Carriers' Association. "Vessel Rosters." www.lcaships.com/wp-content/uploads/2013/03/VESSEL-ROSTERS-PART-II.pdf

2. *Ibid.*

3. U.S. Coast Guard (Department of Transportation). "Marine Casualty Report: SS *Edmund Fitzgerald*; Sinking on November 10, 1975 with Loss of Life in Lake Superior. Report Number 16732/64216." Washington D.C.: U.S. Coast Guard. July 26, 1977. www.uscg.mil/hq/cg5/cg545/docs/boards/edmundfitz.pdf

4. *Ibid.*

5. *Ibid.*

6. *Ibid.*

7. Hultquist, Thomas. R, and Michael R. Dutter and David J. Schwab. "Reexamination of the 9–10 November 1975 "*Edmund Fitzgerald*" Storm Using Today's Technology." Bulletin of the American Meteorological Society. Boston: American Meteorological Society. December 16, 2005. http://journals.ametsoc.org/doi/pdf/10.1175/BAMS-87-5-607

8. *Ibid.*

9. U.S. Coast Guard (Department of Transportation). "Marine Casualty Report: SS *Edmund Fitzgerald*; Sinking on November 10, 1975 with Loss of Life in Lake Superior. Report Number 16732/64216." Washington D.C.: U.S. Coast Guard. July 26, 1977. www.uscg.mil/hq/cg5/cg545/docs/boards/edmundfitz.pdf

The Canadian Great Lakes Fleet

1. Boatnerd.com. "Great Lakes Fleet Photo Gallery." Port Huron: Boatnerd. 2014. www.boatnerd.com/pictures/fleet/

2. Lake Carriers' Association. 2012 Statistical Annual Report of Lake Carrier's Association. "Vessel Rosters." www.lcaships.com/wp-content/uploads/2013/03/VESSEL-ROSTERS-PART-II.pdf

3. Canadian Shipowners' Association. "Our Vessels, Innovation and Investment." 2015. http://shipowners.ca/industryVessels.html

4. Algoma Central Corporation. "Tour the Equinox Class." 2012. www.algonet.com/Business−Units/Domestic−Shipping/Fleet−Renewal/Equinox−Class/Tour−the−Equinox−Class/

5. The St. Lawrence Seaway Management Company. "Introducing the Great Lakes/St. Lawrence Seaway System (brochure)." www.seaway.ca/en/pdf/overview_brochure.pdf

John D. Leitch

1. Boatnerd.com. "−− *John D. Leitch* −− (Canadian Century 1967 − 2002)." Port Huron: Boatnerd. 2015. www.boatnerd.com/pictures/fleet/johnleitch.htm

2. Algoma Central Corporation. "John D. Leitch." 2015. www.algonet.com/Business−Units/Domestic−Shipping/Self−Unloaders/description/item/57?name=John+D.+Leitch

3. *Ibid.*

4. *Ibid.*

5. *Ibid.*

6. Boatnerd.com. "−− *John D. Leitch* −− (Canadian Century 1967 − 2002)." Port Huron: Boatnerd. 2015. www.boatnerd.com/pictures/fleet/johnleitch.htm

7. *Ibid.*

8. National Transportation Safety Board. "Marine Accident Brief: Collision of Canadian Bulk Carrier *John D. Leitch* with Law Enforcement Vessel." May 28, 2013. Washington D.C.: National Transportation Safety Board. www.ntsb.gov/investigations/AccidentReports/Reports/MAB1309.pdf

9. *Ibid.*

About Salties

1. Boatnerd.com. "Foreign Ship Data & Photo Gallery: 2014 Season." Port Huron: Boatnerd. www.boatnerd.com/pictures/salty/

2. *Ibid.*

3. *Ibid.*

4. *Ibid.*

5. *Ibid.*

6. Largestshipsintheworld.com "*Knock Nevis, Seawise Giant, Happy Giant, Jahre Viking, Mount.*" 2014. www.largestshipintheworld.com/largest_ships_in_the_world/knock_nevis_seawise_giant_h.php

Federal Elbe

1. Boatnerd.com. "Foreign Ship Data & Photo Gallery: 2014 Season." Port Huron: Boatnerd. www.boatnerd.com/pictures/salty/

2. Fed Nav. "*Federal Elbe*." 2015. www.fednav.com/en/fleet/federal-elbe

3. *Ibid.*

4. *Ibid.*

5. *Ibid.*

6. *Ibid.*

7. *Ibid.*

8. *Ibid.*

9. Marine Metallurgical Consultants, Ltd. "Experience, Structural Failures." 2012. www.hughesmarine.co.uk/experience.html

About Tugboats

1. Gilchrist, Tom. "Tugboat to hit waterways again." *Bay City Times*. June 4, 2007. http://articles.southbendtribune.com/2007-06-04/news/26782913_1_tugboat-engine-vessel

2. Riedel, Franz A. *Commercial Ships on the Great Lakes: A Photo Gallery*. Hudson: Enthusiast Books. 2005.

Edna G.

1. Lake County Historical Society. "*Edna G.* Tugboat." 2015. http://lakecountyhistoricalsociety.org/museums/view/edna-g.-tugboat

2. *Ibid.*

3. *Ibid.*

4. *Ibid.*

5. *Ibid.*

6. *Ibid.*

7. Gardner, Dennis. *Minnesota Treasures: Stories Behind the State's Historic Places*. St. Paul: Minnesota Historical Society Press. 2004.

8. Minnesota State Historical Society. "Lake Superior Shipwrecks. Madeira: Description of Wreck Event." 2015. www.mnhs.org/places/nationalregister/shipwrecks/madeira/maddwe.php

9. *Ibid.*

10. *Ibid.*

About the Coast Guard

1. United States Coast Guard. "About Us: U.S. Coast Guard Aircraft and Cutters." 2015. www.uscg.mil/datasheet/

2. *Ibid.*

3. Noble, Denis. "Great Lakes: A Brief History of U.S. Coast Guard Operations." Coast Guard Bicentennial Series. 1990. www.uscg.mil/history/articles/GreatLakes.pdf

4. U.S. Life-Saving Service Heritage Association. "Power/Motor Lifeboats." 2015. http://uslife-savingservice.org/lifesavers-duties-equipment/powermotor-lifeboats/

5. Blume, Kenneth J. "Disaster on the Mississippi: The Sultana Explosion, April 27, 1865 (review)" *Civil War History.* December 1997 https://muse.jhu.edu/login?auth=0&type=summary&url=/journals/civil_war_history/v043/43.4.blume.pdf

6. U.S. Coast Guard. "Timeline of Coast Guard Operational History." 2015. www.uscg.mil/lantarea/docs/Timeline of Coast Guard Organizational History.pdf

7. U.S. Coast Guard. "Coast Guard at War." 2014. www.uscg.mil/history/articles/h_CGatwar.asp

8. U.S. Coast Guard. "Frequently Asked Questions: In what wars and conflicts did personnel from the Coast Guard or one of its predecessors serve in and what were the casualties in each?" 2014. www.uscg.mil/history/faqs/wars.asp

9. Canney, Donald. "Rum War: The U.S. Coast Guard and Prohibition." Coast Guard Bicentennial Series. 1990. www.uscg.mil/history/articles/RumWar.pdf

10. *Ibid.*

USCGC *Mackinaw*

1. U.S. Coast Guard. "USCGC *Mackinaw* (WLBB 30), Icebreaking." 2014. www.uscg.mil/d9/cgcMackinaw/icebreaking.asp

2. U.S. Coast Guard. "Characteristics of USCGC *MACKINAW* (WLBB-30)." 2014. www.uscg.mil/d9/cgcMackinaw/characteristics.asp

3. *Ibid.*

4. *Ibid.*

5. *Ibid.*

6. *Ibid.*

7. Grand Haven Coast Guard Festival. "Home." 2015. www.coastguardfest.org

8. Chuck Hawley, John Rousmaniere, Ralph Naranjo and Sheila McCurdy. U.S. Sailing. "Inquiry into the Chicago Yacht Club–Race to Mackinac Capsize and Fatalities." December, 2014. http://media.ussailing.org/AssetFactory.aspx?vid=16940

9. *Ibid*.

10. *Ibid*.

About Tall Ships
1. Sail Training. "Tall Ships Challenge, Pacific Coast 2014." www.sailtraining.org/tallships/2014pacific/TSC2014index.php

2. Sail Training. "Tall Ships Challenge, Great Lakes 2013." www.sailtraining.org/tallships/2013greatlakes/

The *Bounty*
1. The Royal Navy National Museum. "The Mutiny on HMS *Bounty*." 2002. www.royalnavalmuseum.org/info_sheets_bounty.htm

2. National Transportation and Safety Board. "Marine Accident Brief: Sinking of Tall Ship *Bounty*." Washington D.C.: National Transportation and Safety Board. www.ntsb.gov/investigations/AccidentReports/Reports/MAB1403.pdf

3. *Ibid*.

4. *Ibid*.

5. *Ibid*.

6. *Ibid*.

Shipwrecks and Accidents
1. Great Lakes Shipwreck Museum. "Great Lakes Shipwrecks." 2015. www.shipwreckmuseum.com/great-lakes-shipwrecks-6/

2. Thompson, Mark L. *Graveyard of the Great Lakes*. Detroit: Wayne State University Press. 2004. http://wsupress.wayne.edu/books/detail/graveyard-lakes

3. Hennepin, Louis. *A Description of Louisiana*. New York: J.G. Shea. 1800. Accessed via the Internet Archive: https://archive.org/details/descriptionoflou00henn

4. Hennepin, Louis. *A new discovery of a vast country in America, extending above four thousand miles, between New France & New Mexico; with a description of the Great lakes, cataracts, rivers, plants, and animal*. Lon-

don: Henry Bonwicke. 1699. Accessed via the Internet Archive: https://archive.org/details/newdiscoveryofva12henn

5. Great Lakes Exploration Group. "La Salle–*Griffon* Project." http://greatlakesexploration.org/about.htm

6. Nelson, Daniel. "Ghost Ships of the War of 1812." *National Geographic*. March 1983. http://archives.ubalt.edu/swe/pdf/8A-2-25.pdf

7. Blake, Erica. "*Fitzgerald* wreck site gets added protection." Toledo Blade. February 8, 2006. Accessed via The Internet Archive Way-back Machine: http://web.archive.org/web/20060224005347/ http://toledoblade.com/apps/pbcs.dll/article?AID=/20060208/ NEWS19/602080406/-1/NEWS

8. The *Hamilton* and *Scourge* National Historic Site. "Underwater Archaeology." 2015. www.hamilton-scourge.hamilton.ca/ underwater-archaeology.asp

9. Hastings County Historical Society. "Rescuing HMS *Speedy*." Hastings County Historical Society Outlook. January, 2014, Issue 285. Belleville (Ontario): Hastings County Historical Society. http://hastingshistory.ca/ outlook/outlook_2014-01_issue285.pdf

10. *Ibid*.

11. Vyhnak, Carola. "One man's quest to recover artifacts from Lake Ontario shipwreck brings little-known part of Canada's heritage to light." *Toronto Star*. August 18, 2012. www.thestar.com/news/ canada/2012/08/18/one_mans_quest_to_recover_artifacts_from_lake_ ontario_shipwreck_brings_littleknown_part_of_canadas_heritage_to_ light.html

12. Great Lakes Shipwreck Society. "The *Comet* – Lost in 1875." 2015. www.shipwreckmuseum.com/comet

13. Gillham, Skip. "Shipwreck: *Mataafa*." *Mariners' Weather Log*. Wash-ington D.C.: National Oceanographic and Atmospheric Administration. Volume 50, No. 3. December 2006. www.vos.noaa.gov/MWL/dec_06/ shipwreck.shtml

14. LeMay, Konnie. "The *Mataafa* Blow: Stormy Horror of 1905." *Lake Superior Magazine*. October 1, 2005. www.lakesuperior.com/the-lake/ maritime/the-mataafa-blow-stormy-horror-of-1905/

15. Minnesota State Historical Society. "Lake Superior Shipwrecks. *Madeira*: Description of Wreck Event." 2015.

16. *Ibid*.

17. Longacre, Glenn V. "The Christmas Tree Ship: Captain Herman E. Schuenemann and the Schooner *Rouse Simmons*." *Prologue*. Winter, 2006. www.archives.gov/publications/prologue/2006/winter/christmas-tree.html

18. *Ibid*.

19. Port Washington Historical Society. "1860 Lighthouse and Light Station Museum." 2014. www.portwashingtonhistoricalsociety.org/lightstation.htm

20. Lynx Images. "Superior Shoal: The Underwater Mountain & Vanished Ships." 2015. www.lynximages.com/shoal.htm

21. *Eastland* Disaster Historical Society and Meredith Hodge. "What Happened?" 2015. www.eastlanddisaster.org/history/what-happened

22. Mining Awareness Plus. "The Sinking of the SS *Daniel J. Morrell* on Lake Huron, November 29, 1966." 2013. http://miningawareness.wordpress.com/2013/11/29/the-sinking-of-the-ss-daniel-j-morrell-on-lake-huron-november-29-1966/

23. Hale, Dennis. *Sole Survivor: Dennis Hale's Own Story*. Lakeshore Charters & Marine Explorations, Inc. 2002.

24. *Ibid*.

25. U.S. Coast Guard. "SAR Program Information." 2014. www.uscg.mil/hq/cg5/cg534/SAR_Program_Info.asp

26. Hale, Dennis. Sole Survivor: Dennis Hale's Own Story. Lakeshore Charters & Marine Explorations, Inc. 2002.

27. U.S. Coast Guard (Department of Transportation). "Marine Casualty Report: SS *Edmund Fitzgerald*; Sinking on November 10, 1975 with Loss of Life in Lake Superior. Report Number 16732/64216." Washington D.C.: U.S. Coast Guard. July 26, 1977. www.uscg.mil/hq/cg5/cg545/docs/boards/edmundfitz.pdf

28. Hultquist, Thomas. R, and Michael R. Dutter and David J. Schwab. "Reexamination of the 9–10 November 1975 "*Edmund Fitzgerald*" Storm Using Today's Technology." *Bulletin of the American Meteorological Society*. Boston: American Meteorological Society. December 16, 2005. http://journals.ametsoc.org/doi/pdf/10.1175/BAMS-87-5-607

29. The Great Lakes Shipwreck Museum. "The Fateful Journey." 2015. www.shipwreckmuseum.com/the-fateful-journey-62/

A Few Especially Beautiful Ships

1. Boatnerd.com. "Great Lakes Fleet Page Vessel Feature -- *Edward L. Ryerson*." Port Huron: Boatnerd. 2015. www.boatnerd.com/pictures/fleet/elr.htm

2. Boatnerd.com. "Great Lakes Fleet Page Vessel Feature -- *Alpena*." Port Huron: Boatnerd. 2015. www.boatnerd.com/pictures/fleet/alpena.htm

History of Lake Freighter Design

1. Minnesota Historical Society. "Minnesota's Lake Superior Shipwrecks: History and Development of Great Lakes Water Craft (adapted from the National Register's Multiple Property Documentation "Minnesota's Lake Superior Shipwrecks A.D. 1650–1945" by Patrick Labadie, Brina J. Agranat and Scott Anfinson). 2014. www.mnhs.org/places/nationalregister/shipwrecks/mpdf/mpdf2.php

2. Thompson, Mark L. *Graveyard of the Great Lakes*. Detroit: Wayne State University Press. 2004. http://wsupress.wayne.edu/books/detail/graveyard-lakes

Photo Credits

Cover photo (ship image): American Integrity, by Peter Markham.

Kenneth Bailey: 77 (inset), 79 **Fednav: 122–123, Chief Petty Officer Alan Haraf/U.S. Coast Guard:** 67 **Michelle Hill/U.S. Army Corps of Engineers:** 13 (top two), 59, 89, 97, 108–109, 127, 146–147 **T. Johengen/National Oceanographic and Atmospheric Administration:** 87 (inset) **Cathy Kohring:** 69 (main) **Library of Congress:** 153 (bottom), 165 **Peter Markham:** 13 (bottom), 15, 17, 21, 23, 25, 27, 29, 31, 35, 37, 41 (all), 49, 51, 55, 91, 95, 99, 104–105, 107, 113, 121, 131 **National Oceanographic and Atmospheric Administration:** 161 (top) **Brett Ortler:** 5, 47 **Kayli Schaaf:** 200 U.S. **Army Corps of Engineers:** 33, 57 (main), 93, 115, 155 U.S. **Coast Guard:** 69 (inset), 133, 136–137, 139, 145 **Brandon Westberg:** 55

The following (unmodified) photos are licensed per a Creative Commons 2.0 Generic Attribution license, which is available here: http://creativecommons.org/licenses/by/2.0/

Page 57 (inset), "Ships and the International Bridge." Flickr User Shannon Molerus; www.flickr.com/photos/clairity/203741724

Page 65, "Views from Navy Pier in Chicago." Flickr User Loco Steve; www.flickr.com/photos/locosteve/5177041040

Page 71, "Drummond Island Ferry." Flickr User Otisourcat; www.flickr.com/photos/22257034@N00/2195230490

Page 75, "Huron Lightship." Flickr User Jayson Ignacio; www.flickr.com/photos/xjaysonx/4877618913/

Page 77 (main), "Great Lakes freighter passes Detroit." Flickr User Andrea_44; www.flickr.com/photos/8431398@N04/3620727642

Page 100–101, "Indiana Harbor Coming Atch Ya!" Flickr User Randen Pederson; www.flickr.com/photos/chefranden/2681471716

Page 118–119, "Zealand Beatrix – Bulk Carrier." Flickr User Rachel Kramer; www.flickr.com/photos/rkramer62/9325170299/

Page 128–129, "Edna G Tug Boat, Two Harbors," Flickr User Steve Moses; www.flickr.com/photos/smoses/3392305452/

Page 141, "U.S. Brig Niagara." Flickr User Bruce Guenter; www.flickr.com/photos/10154402@N03/9729816245/

Page 142–143, "317/366: The Bounty." Flickr User Magic Madzik; www.flickr.com/photos/cefeida/3093899387/

Page 153, "Equipping nine boats at dock." City of Thunder Bay Archives; www.flickr.com/photos/thunderbayarchives/8414656304

Page 161 (bottom), "20111121 65 St. Mary's Challenger, Milwaukee, Wisconsin." Flickr User David Wilson; www.flickr.com/photos/davidwilson1949/6447897125/

Page 162–163, "Whale Back." Flickr User Randen Peterson; www.flickr.com/photos/chefranden/250995463

Page 85 (main), "Looking backwards into the Eisenhower Lock, from the eastern side." Flickr User James W. Tuttle; www.flickr.com/photos/reivax/246695891

Page 85 (inset), "Exiting the Eisenhower Lock." Flickr User James W. Tuttle; https://www.flickr.com/photos/reivax/246695790/

About the Author

Brett Ortler is an editor at Adventure Publications. He is the author of *Minnesota Trivia Don'tcha Know!*, *The Fireflies Book* and *The Mosquito Book*. His essays, poems and other work appear widely, including in *Salon*, *The Good Men Project*, *The Nervous Breakdown*, *Living Ready* and in a number of other venues in print and online. He lives in the Twin Cities with his wife and their young children.